INNOVATION IS UGLY

TINA LAMBERT

INNOVATION

IS

UGLY

**PRACTICAL ADVICE TO HELP YOU
SUCCEED AGAINST THE ODDS**

ELDEST daughter
PRESS

ISBN (print): 979-8-218-63343-1
ISBN (ebook): 979-8-218-63344-8

For rights and permissions, please contact:
innovationisugly@gmail.com

Book design & typesetting by InsideStudio26.com
All illustrations are the original creations of Nate Fakes
Cover illustrations © Istry Istry, Shutterstock, and Grafissimo, iStock

*To my **daughter**,*
who bought me this laptop
as a Christmas gift six years ago, so I could write this book.
I just started.
This laptop sucks now.
*But she's still **amazing**.*

THE MANDATORY MEANINGFUL QUOTE PAGE

I never lose. I either win or learn.

— Nelson Mandela
(and innovators everywhere?)

A BUSINESS BOOK FOR PEOPLE WHO DON'T LIKE BUSINESS BOOKS

After 20 hard years in innovation, I started what can only be described as a rage journal.

Here's how it went. I'd come home at night *furious* about having yet another circular conversation about innovation with senior executives who Just. Didn't. Get. It. I'd then pour that furious energy into writing down all the things I knew to be true about innovation that I wished I could explain.

Eventually, those explosions of frustration became more than just a journal written in a lot of angry capital letters with an excessive use of underlining. I started seeing the potential to organize my rants into chapters. They became this book. As you'll see, it's a product of passion, frustration, and love. Because, at the end of the day, I still truly *love* innovation, even when it tries to break me.

This is a book about how *hard* product innovation is. It's about how many executives don't understand innovation and think it's things like "fun" and "soft" and "optional." Most importantly, this book is about how to overcome the most painful parts of innovation ... based on over 25 years of me screwing it up and learning the hard way.

I wrote this book for myself, to capture what I've learned. It was cathartic. I also wrote it for innovators everywhere. It's for innovators just getting started who feel overwhelmed by the conflicting direction they are getting; innovators who are getting no direction at all and don't know where to start; innovators who sometimes feel hopeless but aren't fed up yet, like me; and innovators who have been doing this as long as I have, who just want to feel heard. Some of the chapters are about the theory of innovation, and some have specific instructions on how to do different parts of the job.

But this book is also for senior executives. Those of you who want *and need* to understand what is required to give innovation half a chance at survival. Those who feel like they must prioritize the short term consistently over the long term, effectively shooting their innovators in the foot and then asking them to run. Those who don't know how to build a successful innovation engine on their business but wish they did.

BUSINESS BOOKS SUCK

But I had one problem. I *hate* business books.

Business books are so serious. And so dull. And so repetitive. No fun at all. I've always thought of business books as something for bored executives who sit in glass-encased corner offices. They stack them on their desks in plain sight, hoping you'll ask about them. They quote them in their incredibly formulaic town hall presentations.

I've received so many business books over the years as gifts from well-meaning senior leaders. Then comes the social dance of pretending to have read them. Or worse, being forced to actually read them for a "team discussion."

I usually can't get past the preface. Imprisoned by their own predict-ability, business authors rarely inspire me or tell me something I don't know already. I feel like I'm back in school, learning about the distant past instead of what might be possible in the future. How many times can we read about the same old overused case studies?

I'm sure you've had the same experience – it can't just be me.

So, I set out to write something different. It turns out business books need innovation too.

I wanted to capture the reality of product innovation: the good, the bad, and the ugly. I wanted to speak to you, the reader, on my own terms, like a human being rather than a know-it-all lecturer. And I'm a sarcastic human being, who tells it like it is. So, I wanted to be honest and down to earth, casting aside the formality of traditional writing. We are all so busy; who has time for boring business books?

This is a business book that *I* would like to read. It has satisfyingly short chapters, so you get to stop whenever you want.

It also has "snack breaks." These are very short thoughts (one to five pages) that act as a breather between chapters. To be honest, they are mostly rants (I love a good rant).

I tried to design this book to be read in any order you want. So, feel free to skip to the parts you are most curious about first. Or skip past the parts you don't care about. I also wanted to avoid repetition, so instead of explaining concepts over and over again, I will reference the relevant chapter, so you can look it up. That way, if you are skipping around, you can jump to the right section quickly.

I hope I've succeeded in offering something a little different, something that entertains and provokes. If not, by all means, please give your copy to a bored executive.

THIS IS ABOUT PRODUCT INNOVATION

I have been working in product innovation for over 25 years. I've spent most of that time in food and beverage innovation and especially in snack foods (which have a fast pace of innovation!). In *Outliers,* Malcolm Gladwell argues that in order to become an expert in any field, you need about 10,000 hours of practice. I have had about 50,000 hours so far. This is my comfort zone (even though it's uncomfortable a lot of the time).

So, this book is not about process innovation or any buzzy phrases like "commercial innovation." It's not some consultant's broad (and dumb) definition of innovation that includes all-work-done-by-everyone-at-your-company. This book is not about technology breakthroughs. I am not going to mention robot delivery services or AI (again).

But – and it's a big but – I bet, regardless of where you sit on the spectrum of innovation, you'll find insights in this book that will help you. The truth is, when I look at failure in innovation, the same problems pop up again and again. Do you work in service innovation? Marketing technology innovation? Retail innovation? I bet you'll find concepts here that resonate. Corporate America has similar pressures across industries and channels, after all. And when we're under pressure, human behavior is predictable.

YOUR EMERGENCY EXIT SUMMARY

Speaking of pressure, did your manager buy you this book? I hope not.

I hope you are reading this because you are passionate about innovation … or about learning about innovation. I don't want anyone to be *forced* to read this.

About 10 years ago, some of my closest friends *forced* me to go to a haunted house. I am TERRIFIED of haunted houses. Not because I lack bravery, but because I am very suspicious of the kind of people who enjoy bringing the stuff of nightmares to life in a confined space. Isn't there enough to be frightened of in this world already? So, after being forcibly dragged inside by friends, who were all shrieking "You'll like it!" I made it through just three rooms of gore-filled murder scenes and one slow-limping bloody man "chasing" us with an axe before confidently pushing my way through the emergency exit door.

Sooo, here's *your* emergency exit door for this book.

If you *really* don't want to read this, the next four pages hold a list of key points that will allow you to *pretend* you did … effectively fooling your boss and coworkers.

PART I: MISCONCEPTIONS

CHAPTER	TALK POINTS TO CONVINCE OTHERS YOU READ THIS CHAPTER
ONE: WHY Innovation Is Ugly (Not Fun)	Innovation isn't "fun." It's a battle! It can fail in SO. MANY. WAYS.
TWO: What Innovation Success Really Looks Like (It May Surprise You)	Innovation doesn't drive base growth. But it will stack up over time like the shoes do in your closet.
THREE: Innovation Prioritization: Bigger Isn't Better, but Medium Is the Worst	Big innovation is hard. Small innovation is, well, small. But medium innovation is the WORST.
FOUR: Profitable Innovation Matters. It Has to Be Cute	Should we expect innovation margins to be higher than the rest of the business? In this chapter, I argue with myself.
FIVE: Let's Stop Lying About Our Innovation Forecasts	Innovators lie about their new item forecasts. A lot. It might help them get their plans approved, but it sure doesn't help the product succeed.
SIX: Popping Candy and Breakfast Pizza? Creativity Isn't About Being Weird	I explain why thinking inside a box (with creative guardrails) is easier. Also, Americans love pizza. Maybe too much. And they think it's "creative" for some reason.

PART II: THE "FUN" PART

CHAPTER	TALK POINTS TO CONVINCE OTHERS YOU READ THIS CHAPTER
SEVEN: What the Duck Do You Own? (Points of Difference)	Consumers better ducking care about your idea, and they will if your point of difference is strong.
EIGHT: Dumb Brain-storms Lead to Dumb Ideas	Brainstorms require more planning than you might think in order to generate unique ideas.
NINE: Innovation Island	If you send all of your innovators to an island, they will get drunk and forget they're trying to make you money. Fun for them – bad for business.
TEN: Innovation Is Already Agile: Keep Stealing Ideas from Design Thinking	Blah blah insights from design thinking. Yes, it's overhyped in innovation right now, but there are some aspects we can all learn from.
ELEVEN: Say Less! Writing Simple, Strong Innovation Concepts	Say Less. The end.

PART III: LONG-TERM PLANNING

CHAPTER	TALK POINTS TO CONVINCE OTHERS YOU READ THIS CHAPTER
TWELVE: Nailing Innovation Pacing and Mix	Creating a three-year innovation calendar with the right mix of projects needed for your category – big, medium, and small – is the route to sustainable success. Don't create a funnel – it's a dumb theory.
THIRTEEN: Innovation Strategies That Resist the Winds of Change	Creating an innovation strategy is a process and should be treated as one. This chapter has a crapload of steps as a result because you need to identify the target, focus areas, objectives, pacing, and guardrails for your innovation program at least once a year.
FOURTEEN: Stop Yammering About "TRENDS"	Trends are either long-term or they aren't trends.
FIFTEEN: Pivot Around Barriers	When you hit a wall in innovation, pivot around it. Never give up, unless the flow chart says to.
SIXTEEN: Don't Let Renovation and Cost Savings Bring Innovation Down	Innovation, cost savings, and renovation are *all* necessary and deliver different business outcomes. Stop asking them to compete, stupid executive.
SEVENTEEN: Execution Matters … MOST	Strong distribution + strong trade support + strong advertising support = *innovation success*. Even if your idea is cheesy.

EIGHTEEN: Trolls at the Gate: How to Convince Them to Let You Pass	There are trolls out there guarding the launch gate, and they work for not-so-small-mart. You need to work out how to convince them to let you pass.
NINETEEN: The Boring Business Chapter: The Fundamentals of Innovation Success	If you are using this emergency exit plan, you would have skipped this one, and it's fine to admit that.
TWENTY: A Graceful Exit	We all fail at some point. Read this if you want to know what to do. I get weirdly sappy in this one.

Oh, wait. Are you still reading? Great, then let's get to it.

Deep breath Be warned: What you are about to read isn't always pretty. Buy hey, at least there's no bloody man with a slow limp.

PART I:

MISCONCEPTIONS

THE TRUTH ABOUT INNOVATION
AND WHAT WE'RE DOING WRONG

– SNACK BREAK –

DON'T YOU DARE SAY INNOVATION IS FUN!

I'm going to start this book with a plea.

DON'T say innovation is fun. Please.

People who say innovation is fun have never led innovation. Saying innovation is "fun" is a smooth dismissal of innovation as a "creative" space for soft, dumb, "creative" people.

Innovation is hard. Innovators have to be hard too, and this book will show you why.

You really shouldn't need me to tell you that innovation is hard; the failure rates should speak for themselves. Depending on the data source you use, between 50% and 80% of all innovations fail. The true rate of failure is higher than outsiders might think ... because so many innovation ideas die *way* before they make it to market. The benchmark for project success is making it to market and lasting for at least a few years, and that is incredibly rare.

Up against odds like that, a business leader will likely want to minimize risk in every way possible. The temptation is to try and understand *all* the variables and systematically test them for signs of weakness. But innovation also needs to be fast. And reactive. The competition isn't sitting still and politely waiting for you to check all your boxes before you make a move. A typical innovation challenge is filled with paradoxes like this.

I need you to be silly fast but minimize risk.
I need you to produce huge incremental revenue with minimal investment.
I need something that differentiates itself in the market but which runs smoothly in our existing manufacturing plants.
I need you to deliver a premium product that's good value but also reaps high profits, please?

We innovators are often chasing an unattainable ideal. In my mind, innovation is like swimming. When you learn to swim, it's hard. You need training from people with experience. But once you start to get the hang of it and the fear fades, you are just playing with your friends.

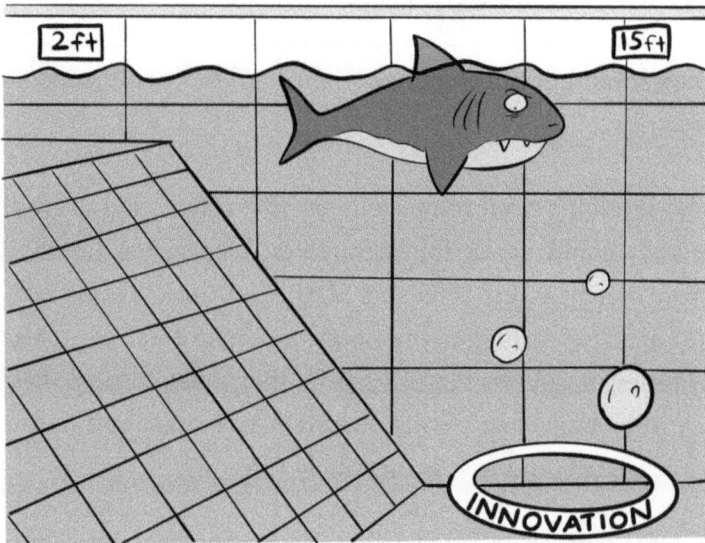

When an innovation team is working well, it's just like that. You're diving into the deep end of the pool … with your buddies cheering you on. I believe innovation is allowed to be hard as long as it is equally fun. Otherwise, your innovators are just, well, drowning.

Good thing innovation is so fun? Right, guys???

Only us innovators can use that word! Don't underestimate how hard we are kicking to keep things afloat.

CHAPTER ONE

WHY INNOVATION IS UGLY (NOT FUN)

Innovation is ugly. Even though it can be fun, it's also incredibly difficult. What makes it so difficult is how often it fails.

And the reason most innovation fails is because there are SO. MANY. potential modes of failure for innovation.

Let's start by breaking the innovation journey into three phases. We start with an idea, then we develop it within our company, then we launch it out into the world. It sounds simple enough, right? But let's consider some of the many things that can go wrong.

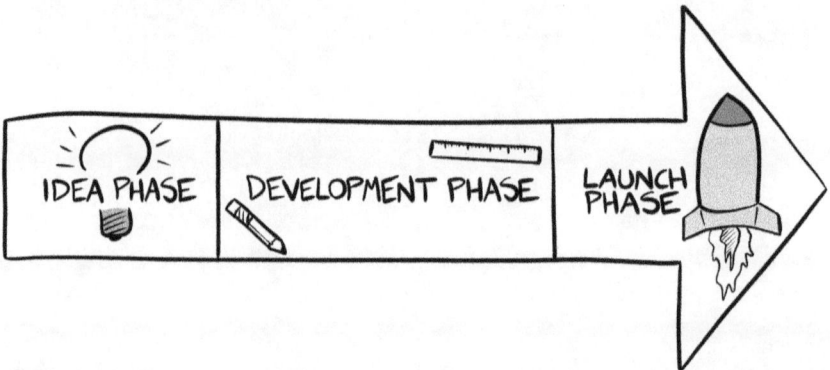

PHASE ONE: YOU NEED A (GOOD) IDEA

Innovations all start with an idea. Unfortunately, a lot of ideas are bad. We'll talk about why creativity is so hard a little later on in Chapter Six (or feel free to jump there now). A good idea will be based on consumer needs and grounded in a consumer insight. And your idea has to be ownable ... meaning no one else can do it quite like your brand or company. Copycat innovation almost always fails unless it is purely aiming to imitate and undercut a leader's price point.

Speaking of price, value is another critical point of failure in this phase. It's important to know from the beginning of an innovation project whether your target consumers and customers will be willing to pay the premium your new idea will require.

PHASE TWO: CAN YOU EVEN MAKE IT?

When I worked on cereal innovation, one of my running jokes with my food scientists was that invisible cereal was one of the best testing ideas we had ever come up with for kids. It summed up a truism in innovation: Often, the best ideas fail because they aren't technically possible. When ideas just can't be made, we often compromise and develop what we *can* make instead of what people actually want. *How about cereal that's not invisible ... but you can make it disappear!* *dad joke groan*

Probably the number-one reason I have killed innovation projects in my career is for financial reasons. I've summarized this on the chart below as "not profitable," but there's a lot to unpack here. You may think of profitability as pricing to cover the costs, but it's also about ensuring a return on any capital investment required *and* the ability to invest in sales and marketing spending to gain distribution and drive sales.

Innovation is, by definition, creating something that's different, and different usually means more expensive, lower scale, and less efficient for manufacturing. If you can't price to cover this, you'll be launching at a lower margin than the rest of your product offerings. Even if you can sell management on getting that out the door, the innovation will be under constant cost pressure from then on, reducing its chances of long-term success.

PHASE THREE: THE RISK IS OUT THERE

Imagine that you brainstorm a good idea, develop an offering that delivers on all its benefits, and, somehow, it makes financial sense; now you can release your baby into the wild. Surely that's the bulk of the work done? Unfortunately not. In launch phase, the risks are less predictable and more out of your control. Can you secure distribution with retailers, wholesalers, and distributors? Or do they think your idea sucks? What if there's no room on store shelves without eliminating something else that's performing well? You have no idea what your competition has been working on all this time; they could launch something similar…or cheaper…or better! Or, even worse (and harder to predict), the market could have shifted. Now your idea is off trend … or you may be launching something ultra-premium into a recession.

Sometimes you manage to survive all of these modes of failure. You feel like you've finally completed the obstacle course only to see your sales numbers whimper in. Your innovation never really becomes popular, and it dies a slow death over one or two years, eventually getting replaced by the next new thing. Innovators have to have a strong stomach.

Ugh. Sounds less fun now, doesn't it?

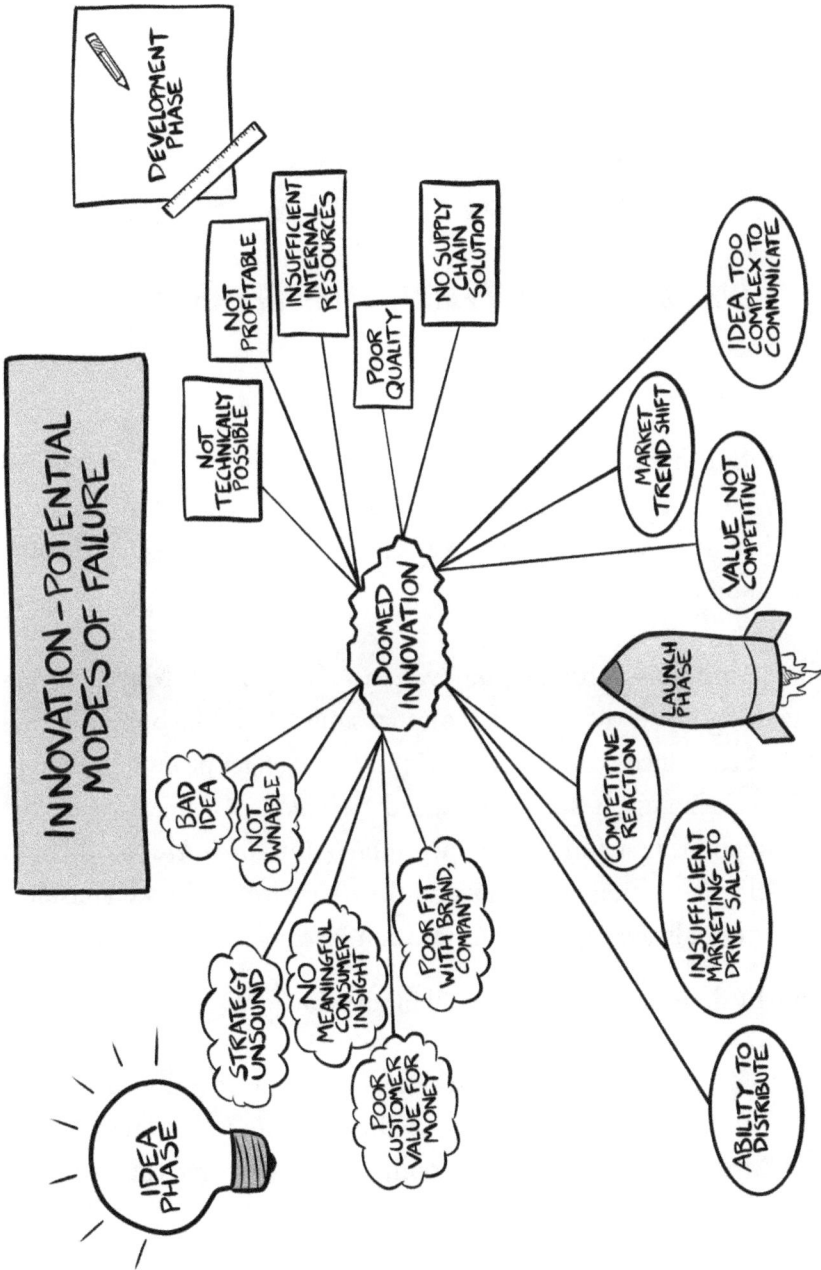

INNOVATION – POTENTIAL MODES OF FAILURE

DEVELOPMENT PHASE

NOT TECHNICALLY POSSIBLE

NOT PROFITABLE

INSUFFICIENT INTERNAL RESOURCES

POOR QUALITY

NO SUPPLY CHAIN SOLUTION

IDEA TOO COMPLEX TO COMMUNICATE

MARKET TREND SHIFT

VALUE NOT COMPETITIVE

DOOMED INNOVATION

BAD IDEA

NOT OWNABLE

STRATEGY UNSOUND

NO MEANINGFUL CONSUMER INSIGHT

POOR FIT WITH BRAND, COMPANY

POOR CUSTOMER VALUE FOR MONEY

IDEA PHASE

COMPETITIVE REACTION

LAUNCH PHASE

INSUFFICIENT MARKETING TO DRIVE SALES

ABILITY TO DISTRIBUTE

– SNACK BREAK –

INNOVATION WON'T FIX YOUR BROKEN BUSINESS

Innovation has lots of different purposes, but I often see executives try to use it in the wrong way. They see a business that is *declining*, and they want to use innovation as the silver bullet to *fix* it, providing growth on a silver platter.

If your business is broken, innovation will *not* fix it. Maybe there's something about your proposition that's outdated. Maybe your brand has lost relevance. Maybe your business is no longer profitable enough to be prioritized. If so, there's a red flag here. You have to fix the fundamentals first and then launch innovation (or at *least* fix them in parallel to launching new innovation). Otherwise, the broken business will almost always break the innovation instead.

But why do broken businesses kill innovation?

- **Your internal team is distracted.** Everyone is really busy trying to fix the *problem* that is a declining business. No one has time to prioritize your innovation, so you can't get the resources required to be successful.

- **You can't get funding.** Companies want to invest capital and marketing dollars in the *growing* parts of their business that they feel will generate the highest returns – the last thing they want to do is take risks on a part of the business that is already not performing. So, they probably won't give you much money to support your new item launch. Also, if the business is indeed broken, chances are your budget is tight right now.

- **You can't get in-market distribution** because your retailer and/or distributor is frustrated with your poor base business performance, and they're not interested in betting on you further. They are focused on the parts of their business that are growing, just like your company.

- **You can't draw high-value consumers** to your brand, shelf, or business because your current offering doesn't appeal to them (maybe *that's* why your business is declining). As a result, the consumers you want to attract never even see or hear about this new innovation (and therefore don't buy it).

The innovation failures that weigh heaviest on me in my career are the ones that were wonderful, meaningful ideas for consumers that I launched for struggling brands. Even with the *best* idea in the category, and an *amazing* product that delivered on that idea, some of those innovations never really had a chance to succeed. They were doomed from their inception. They struggled for the reasons I just outlined, and no amount of success in product innovation development could overcome the drag of a broken business.

So, when thinking about using innovation for growth, consider your business situation. Is it a startup? Is it an old brand that needs something fresh and new? Is this a brand or category that's growing really fast and you want to keep pace with others? All of those could be *great* situations for innovation, if the business is healthy. The key question is whether innovation is the solution to a problem or one of several drivers of growth.

Now, let's think about the opposite – how growing brands can help support innovation. Growing businesses are a priority for their parent companies and usually also a priority for investment. They're often able to secure incremental shelf or distribution placements because their retailers and distributors are happy with them. That incremental distribution will make your innovation even more incremental (more incremental = more growth!). Growing businesses are also constantly bringing in new households, meaning more consumers will know about your innovation. Base business growth drives innovation.

All of that support and momentum matters. Success breeds success. So, try to innovate in your healthiest businesses and brands first, and NEVER use innovation as a "fix."

CHAPTER TWO

WHAT INNOVATION SUCCESS REALLY LOOKS LIKE (IT MAY SURPRISE YOU)

Innovation doesn't drive base growth.

That means it won't drive growth on your original (non-innovation) products.

Whoa! What did I just say?

Let's back up. Why do most people want innovation? Growth, of course. Tons of it, preferably. But the reality is more complicated.

In fact, a lot of the time, when you have a really successful innovation engine, your company's original offerings will experience flat sales growth, or they may even be slightly down due to cannibalization.

(Do I have *no* good news? Well, the book title should have warned you. :))

This is an ugly truth about innovation and one that I find executives *almost never understand.* When the analysts see that the core business is flat and the growth is purely due to the innovation, they panic (you can tell because they write that in ALL CAPS in an email). Then an executive does an about-face and says, "We should focus more on the core business and stop doing so much innovation."

face palm

But they are missing out on the long game. After 25 years of driving growth across Fortune 500 food and beverage companies, I'm here to tell you what innovation success can look like:

A successful, long-term innovation program in a healthy company drives compounded growth over time.

It looks like a stacked bar chart, where each year of innovation is stacked up over time, driving profitable, sustainable growth for your business.

INNOVATION GROWTH OVER TIME
(EACH SHADE IS A YEAR'S WORTH OF LAUNCHES)

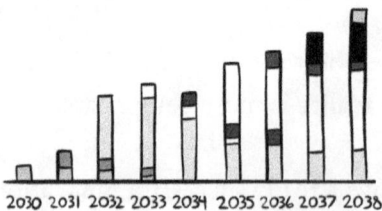

INNOVATION IMPACT ON BASE BUSINESS
(HINT: IT DRIVES GROWTH ON A DECLINING BASE)

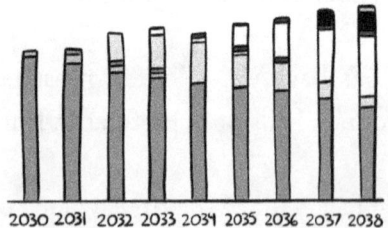

2030 2031 2032 2033 2034 2035 2036 2037 2038   2030 2031 2032 2033 2034 2035 2036 2037 2038

These charts illustrate what I mean. Note that the shades of gray, black and white represent different innovation launches, whereas the large dark gray bar in the chart on the right represents base products (your original business you are innovating on). They both show nine years of innovation because innovation often comes in three-year cycles (with at least one big thing every three years).

First, let's consider the chart on the left:

- **Each year you launch a "class" of innovation.** For example, the class of 2030 (in medium gray) was a "just okay" group of innovations, and none of them lasted longer than three years (which is not that unusual for smaller launches).

- **Some of the classes are going to be bigger (in terms of sales) and some are going to last longer in the market (we call that being "sticky").** For example, the class of 2032 (in light gray) was both. Big and sticky often go hand in hand, although bigger innovation can be riskier too.

- **The stacked bars show that even when *many* individual innovations fail, over nine years, the innovation program drives significant growth.**

Now, let's move to the chart on the right:

- **The exact same 10 years' worth of innovation shown in the chart on the left is shown in the chart on the right, but it's now layered over the performance of the base business.** In this case, I assumed that base business was slowly declining each year, like many stable businesses do.

- **What the chart shows is that a regular stream of innovation, with a good mix of small, medium, and large ideas, will drive total business growth,** even if the base business declines. (We will talk more about what a good mix of innovation is in Chapter Twelve.)

I love using this visual because it is so important for innovators and executives to understand that a successful innovation program *doesn't rely on a 100% success rate.* Each year, you launch a number of new items. Some of them end up as big hits, but a lot of them fail. Typically, with a strong innovation program, I see a class grow in year two, then decline in year three, as those short-term wins lose consumer interest. You can see that, over a nine-year period, I assumed some classes were completely gone by year three and some were long-term successes.

So, success actually lies in consistency. When you have a long-term innovation program focused on consistently launching a good mix of innovation over time – you win. Enough of them stick to overcome those that fail and drive business growth.

As innovation stacks up over time, your original offerings slowly become a lower share of your business. This is COMPLETELY FINE, as long as your innovation is profitable (and if it isn't, it likely won't survive – see Chapter Four).

Let's use a grim analogy.

This concept can be confusing to people, so here's another way to frame it. Think about old-school war, with troops running at other troops across the battlefield. As a leader, you send waves of troops out over time. Some of them fall, and you expect that. But if you have enough, over time, some will get through the other side's defenses, and you'll start to gain ground. Maybe death and destruction isn't the best way to explain innovation growth, but it does sum up what I'm talking about. A successful innovation engine, to some extent, is about not giving up. It's about continuing to push new innovations across the field and into market, while being attacked by your competitors, even when you know some of those innovations won't make it.

And, as you read through this book, you'll learn how to make your troops smarter and more likely to succeed. Hint: training and equipment matter.

Now imagine the opposite. You have troops but you just sit still. You focus only on reinforcing and fortifying your existing position. This is what happens when businesses concentrate all their resources on their core offerings and fail to invest in innovation. Yes, sometimes they build almost impenetrable fortresses.

In this scenario, it may take longer for your opposition to encroach on your territory, but it's inevitable. Your fancy fortress will be tempting to others with a more aggressive strategy. And it's hard to gain ground when you're not moving forward, so how are you growing? The landscape will change around you while you sit in your fortress, and one day you'll wake up and realize it has become irrelevant.

But is this just theory or will it really work, you may ask.

I can assure you, I've seen this approach drive significant growth in healthy brands. Think of the fastest growing established brands in your categories and channels. Chances are, they have a healthy innovation engine behind them. In my industry, I can think of examples from cereal, snack food, and frozen food brands. For example, look at the progress Jimmy Dean® has made over the years, expanding from a sausage brand … to a frozen sandwich brand … to a broad line of breakfast meals and snacks. If you mapped the brand's growth over time, it would likely look very similar to this stacked bar chart.

In many cases, the brands were growing anyway, through smart positioning and advertising. But innovation was the key driver of growth over time.

So, how do you measure this innovation success each year so you know whether you are doing enough?

Leaders are often tempted to focus on the in-year sales vs. that year's target, but that metric won't tell them if they're driving sustainable, long-term growth.

In fact, the biggest problem with focusing on in-year sales as the key deliverable for innovation is that it encourages short-term thinking. It only rewards what happens in the present, with no consideration for whether the team is working on bigger, longer-term projects that will be sticky in market.

I have found the absolute best metric for innovation success is a **three-year innovation rate.** This is the percentage of a company's total revenue that is generated from innovation launched in the past three years.

You can calculate this as follows:

*Total revenue $ **this year** from innovation products launched in **the last three years***

$$\div$$

Total revenue $ from sales this year across the entire business

What's a good target percentage for your three-year innovation rate? My experience in food and beverage says 10-15% is strong. Anything in single digits is weak, and if your percentage approaches 20%, you are probably doing too much innovation (at the expense of your core offerings). However, note that every business model and market is different. In order to set the right target for *your* business, you'll need to do an in-depth analysis of your key competitors, which any scan data provider can help you with. Setting the right target is the first step in creating an innovation engine that will drive the growth you need, so this analysis is worth the time and money.

When it comes to innovation rate, the important thing is to set a target and try to stick to it over time. You want to create an innovation pipeline that keeps you at the same target rate year after year. This rewards your innovation team for launching innovation that sticks in market longer than one year, *and* it forces them to think about innovation as a portfolio, with some smaller items that rotate often and some bigger ideas that last for a while.

If you only launch small, short-term innovation, you'll struggle to launch *enough* to hit your target rate because they never stay in the market long enough. If you launch only big-ticket items, you will have years with nothing new appearing (since you likely can't afford to launch something big every single year). We'll get into this in greater depth in Chapter Twelve, where we'll talk about pacing and mix.

But what if you don't have the money or data to produce a three-year innovation rate?

Don't worry, there is another way to incentivize your team to focus on long-term, compounding innovation growth. You just need to determine what portion of your total business growth needs to come from innovation and set a long-term target.

For example, say you want your total business to grow 3% a year. Where will that come from? Likely some combination of distribution growth, promotional effectiveness, pricing, advertising, innovation, and natural market growth (i.e., trends in your favor). Build a financial bridge that shows how much you want each of these factors to contribute to that. You might decide a third (or 1%) of that growth needs to come from innovation each year. This gives your innovators an ongoing, top-down target. And they can easily convert it into a revenue target and work to build a pipeline against it.

Top-down targets are always better for innovation teams because they help to drive long-term thinking and planning. Rather than just basing this year's innovation growth plan on the projects at hand, the team will be reconciling their current pipeline with what they've been told they need to deliver. It will force them to think ahead and make sure they have enough for next year.

Even without a three-year innovation rate, that simple shift will help you start your journey toward stacking up classes of innovation that will compound over time, driving growth for your business. And, by that, I mean your *total* business, not your base.

A final note to the executives: Be patient and remember that innovation is a long-term investment.

– SNACK BREAK –

FEWER, BIGGER, BETTER? WRONG. (CUT. IT. OUT.)

Nothing makes me more furious than the phrase "fewer, bigger, better" when it comes to innovation.

It's often a mantra for senior leaders. They must learn it at some how-to-sound-like-a-senior-leader camp I've never been invited to. Sometimes, I hear it from consultants who have never worked in the real world.

Concentrating on fewer innovations that are bigger and better is a deeply flawed strategy. Let's consider it in a different context. If you're investing funds for long-term growth, when is <u>fewer</u> ever the right answer? Just think about it for a moment. With your retirement portfolio, are you holding just three good stocks? Putting all your eggs in the biggest and best ones? No, of course not! That would be insanely risky. The only people I know who do this are super young investors who are just playing around on the market because they don't have the funds to invest properly.

Innovation is also an investment in growth, right? So, why would you manage it differently than any other investment portfolio?

The sad truth is that "fewer" is just management's way of saying "we can't afford this" under the guise of "strategy." "This" being investment in a real innovation engine. They are those "super young investors" who don't have the funds and just want to play around with innovation. Or, even worse, they *actually* believe that investing in just a few, giant, risky projects is the right way to go. They expect you to play home run baseball 100% of the time. But, guess what? The top home run hitters often have the most strikeouts each year too! Ouch.

Before we go any further, let's make sure you understand what I mean when I talk about small, medium, and big bet innovations.

Small innovation is close to what your core product offerings are. It might be a new variety, a seasonal or limited-time offering, a new package size, a specific configuration to make that product work in a new channel of business, or an upgraded version of your core. Small innovations are important to have in the mix because they keep your product line fresh, providing news that proves your brand is relevant. An example of a small innovation: the bundle pack created for a club store.

Medium innovation is not small or big. LOL. I'm not actually joking; it's often defined by the edges. These projects often are like small bets but have higher revenue. New varieties of your core offering that will get broad distribution often fit here. An example of a medium innovation: the fourth flavor of your cracker line. These projects might not be small, but they usually aren't very incremental to your business.

Big bet innovations get the addition of the word "bet" to their size because they are more of a gamble. Anytime you are working on something with a lot of incremental revenue, it is probably requiring investment in new manufacturing equipment and a lot of resources to support its development. Big bets should be going after unmet consumer needs and whitespaces for your company. They typically take the longest time to bring from idea to market. An example of a big bet would be an innovation that goes after a whole new category for your company that you don't compete in today. Big bet innovation is rare. Few brands launch big bets *frequently* because of the investment required to make them work. But they are an important part of an innovation strategy if you want to generate significant growth over time.

Obviously, big innovations have an important role in your portfolio. They are the way you change the category you compete in. But big innovation often means big investment in resources, capital, and advertising. And, as we know from the many potential ways to fail described in Chapter One, they don't always work. The reality is that small and medium innovation are much more likely to succeed. That's because they're often closer to your current offering and therefore highly likely to appeal to your core target user. They may drive less incremental growth, but their more reliable profits will keep your business ticking up.

In the same way, a "small ball" strategy (all singles) can win baseball games. Just ask the best baseball manager of all time, Terry Francona (fight me, Yankees' fans). It may not win you a big game against a well-funded team, though. For that, you'll need a few strategic big hits.

So, a good mix will drive you toward your goal – long-term, stacked growth. We'll talk in depth about mix in Chapter Twelve. Don't only swing for the fences, but don't play it safe and load your pipeline with little bunts as they probably won't drive a high enough score over time.

Good pitching also helps. And by good pitching, I mean an excellent project manager, which we'll cover in the snack break after Chapter Fifteen. But that's enough baseball analogies for now.

CHAPTER THREE

INNOVATION PRIORITIZATION: BIGGER ISN'T BETTER, BUT MEDIUM IS THE WORST

Once you start stacking up innovation growth, you may find you don't have enough resources to innovate as much as you want. The number of ideas will start to outweigh the size of your team or your budget. At that point, you'll need to find a way to prioritize.

Innovation prioritization. Ugh. I really believe it's one of the areas of innovation that few get right. It feels impossible sometimes.

There are *so many* tools available for innovation prioritization. And they are all *so* complicated and involve *so* much data input and analysis.

I'm here to tell you that, in my experience, most of them are a WASTE of the same precious resources you are trying to protect through prioritization.

There are companies with prioritization tools that track resource usage (and guess who has to fill those out, your constrained resources). There are complicated algorithms that decide which projects are the most valuable across multiple financial attributes. There are insane scatter plots that attempt to graph your projects. Your analytics-minded team members might even want to create a DIY tool. This usually turns into a overly complicated spreadsheet with all kinds of financial metrics thrown together using subjective measures around high-medium-low resource usage and complexity. And then it spits out a random number. Whaaaat?

At the end of the day, a human executive still has to look at these complex analyses and make a tough decision on what makes the cut and what doesn't. You can't resource every idea you have (and if you can, you probably aren't working on big enough ideas). **And, inevitably, even with all these expensive charts and graphs in front of them, that executive won't want to – or feel able to – decide which things to stop.**

But why do you have too much innovation in the first place?

Sure, in an ideal world, you would create a calendar and pace out exactly how much innovation you need to meet your growth goals and the needs of the market (more about how to do that in Chapter Twelve). But we don't live in an ideal world. You likely have too much innovation because there are lots of different stakeholders demanding it and not enough pushback.

Perhaps a customer demanded something exclusive, your senior leader asked for a pet project as a favor, the marketing team came up with some really cool seasonal items, sales wanted a new value tier item to hit a price point, your competitors launched something everyone thinks is a threat, and the research team developed a new technology and sold it up the management chain. If you had read that last sentence out loud, you would feel the way the most constrained part of your innovation team feels when you don't prioritize ... like they can't catch their breath.

If you have multiple marketing and/or sales teams fighting for the same innovation resources, your prioritization challenge will only get worse. Now you have *internal* competition, and they'll all want their projects prioritized. None of your stakeholders are going to volunteer to have their project stopped when it turns out you don't have enough resources to do it all.

But if you try to do it all and ask your teams to take on too much, everything will move slowly. None of those projects will stay on their timelines.

No prioritization leads to weak pipelines.

Inevitably, you'll get stuck in one of the worst traps innovators fall into: **You'll only work on the thing that needs to launch soonest.** This leads to unsustainable thinking: *What really matters right now is delivering this year! We need to meet this customer demand right now! Forget the future – none of us will still be here in three years anyway, right?* Ooohhh, this last comment gets me heated.

Also, by *not* choosing, your executives *do* choose. And they'll choose small, short-term innovation at the expense of ever launching those big bets that will meaningfully grow your business. You'll get stuck in churn innovation and the most important and groundbreaking projects will be delayed again and again, never given the focus they need to progress.

Well, this all sounds hopeless, doesn't it? I told you at the top of this chapter that none of the prioritization tools in the market will help, so what's an innovator to do?

Kill the middle!

In my experience, the best solution is counterintuitive. You might think the easiest way to make space is to kill all the smallest projects, but there's usually a really good reason you *need* that small stuff for the business. The small projects are incremental growth opportunities with key customers or in key channels. They are tweaks to your product line that keep them relevant to today's consumers. The fact that they are small is obvious, so they should have only been suggested because they were important. (Still, pressure test this to stop anyone from sneaking dumb stuff through.)

As I've shown, you can't kill the big stuff either. Those are the true incremental growth drivers. Yes, they take up TONS of resources, but if you want to have a successful long-term innovation program, you need them in the mix to stack up and create long-term growth.

So, kill the middle. The medium-sized projects usually take up a fair amount of resources, but they won't end up being very incremental to the business. A lot of the time, they're the projects you think you need because you've always done something like that in the past. The middle is the fourth flavor of a cracker line. Sure, someone will think it's delicious, but the world will be okay without it ... everyone likes cheddar anyway! The middle is a channel launch that might not be small, but it's not big enough to be worth the amount of work it will take.

So, how do we choose those middle projects to kill?

Prioritization is still a tough decision. Killing some projects from the middle will be hard, but it's necessary.

And the only tool you need? A simple list. Nothing fancier or more complex than that.

To start, rank order the projects from biggest to smallest in terms of expected ongoing revenue (I say ongoing because year one might vary based on time of launch or distribution build). Honestly, your sales or marketing innovation lead can usually create this list without even having the revenue data in front of them; they know the relative sizes of the projects.

Get that list in front of your decision makers. And then look HARD at the middle with your very best judgy eyes.

Still struggling? If you add a second metric around how profitable each of these innovations are, it will help you choose the middle projects with the lowest business impact. Stop those. Still can't uncap your red pen? Stop the (middle) projects on the lowest-priority part of your business.

However you decide to choose, try not to make it overcomplicated for yourself or your team. Again, if the hard work here is in the analysis, *your decision maker is probably just procrastinating*. Don't be that person.

Do the impossible: Prioritize your innovation. Give your projects the resources they need, and give those resources some breathing room.

CHAPTER FOUR

PROFITABLE INNOVATION MATTERS. IT HAS TO BE CUTE

A few years back, I moved to a new part of the country for my job. I was an empty nester and traveling for work less than I had for years; suddenly I had more free time. New to the community, I also had fewer local connections. Feeling a little alone and aimless, I decided to get a puppy. *My* puppy was, of course, more brilliant and beautiful than all other dogs that have ever graced the earth. That summer, my daughter graduated from college, came home, met my amazing puppy, and suddenly got inspired to get *her own puppy*. So, in case you've lost count, we now had TWO PUPPIES IN ONE HOUSE. That's too many puppies. We referred to them as "tyrants" because they ran the house like a co-dictatorship.

That fall, I got up early one morning and took the puppies for a walk in my pajamas. It had rained hard the night before, so the neighborhood was super muddy. We were cutting through a grassy area when, suddenly, the tyrants looked at each other, instantly developed an evil plan, and took off in a full run ... while still attached (via leashes) to me. They galloped with abandon down a muddy hill, dragging me behind. I describe the experience as a lot like waterskiing – only instead of a boat, I had two autocrat puppies, and instead of water,

I had a muddy hill. I managed to stay on my feet almost all the way down, but once I neared the bottom, I lost all control. Down I went, with a sickening crack. I completely blew my left knee, tearing my MCL and PCL, and I ended up with a terrifying-looking leg brace and crutches for the next three months.

Here's what's wild. I wasn't even mad at the puppies. We didn't promptly give them away. I didn't even yell at them in the moment, while I lay on the ground sobbing and they jumped around me like it was a fun, roll-in-the-mud game. Why? Because puppies are really stinking cute. When we're feeling low, they make us laugh. We love them like they are members of the family. But we would *never* put up with all the shenanigans of puppies (or children) if it wasn't for how cute they are. Nature knows what it's doing with their big eyes and goofy grins.

My point is, there's a payback. We get something out of all the work we put in with puppies.

This is a long, gentle lead-in to get to my point: innovations need to have a payback too. They are also *hard* work. They can also be infuriating. Sometimes, operations and R&D professionals would like to throttle an innovation that is making their job too hard. Innovators – if you want to keep your projects from being sidelined, you need to make sure the business thinks they're cute.

And what's cuter to business people than profit? Not much, in my experience.

That's why profitable innovation matters – often more than having a good idea.

And this can be a problem. People assume "creativity" is the most important attribute of a good innovator. In fact, having spent a

CUTE PUPPIES   CUTE INNOVATION

WE BOTH ATE FOOD FROM THE COUNTER...

(NOTE THE BIG EYES)   (NOTE THE TALL STACK)

great deal of my career surrounded by innovators, **the <u>worst</u> I've ever worked with have been the <u>most</u> creative.** I call them "head in the clouds" innovators. They launch ridiculously creative things that have no foundation in reality. Most of these fail, either because they are too weird or because they aren't financially sustainable. I always say I'm a "practical innovator." My feet are firmly on the ground.

The biggest difference between unsuccessful and successful innovators is not creativity but financial acumen. Successful innovators can build a P&L from scratch and then take it back apart and rebuild it. One time, I found a human error in the manufacturing costs in a project's P&L financials *one hour* before the final launch approval meeting. The error raised our cost by 10 cents a unit, which caused our margin to be unacceptable. I came up with a list of options and made a ton of phone calls. An hour later, we had slightly shrunk the size of the product and cut the sales trade rate. It launched on track. You need innovators who can react quickly to these realities under pressure.

But how do we ensure our innovation is profitable?

Margin targets are the answer.

Financial targets are *critical* for long-term success – and margin is the most important. Innovators therefore need *very* clear expectations for their margins. But clarity on margin targets isn't always easy as there are two different schools of thought on innovation financials. One believes innovation margin should be accretive (higher than the rest of the business). The other thinks that high margin standards hold innovations back.

The question is, exactly *how cute* do you believe a baby innovation has to be?

Let's look at the merits of both sides.

School of thought #1: Innovation should be margin accretive

This means an innovation should be higher margin than the core business offerings, improving a company's gross profit margins. I find the more senior the leader, the more likely this is their argument. Public company boards especially seem to advocate for accretive innovation.

Why? The argument is that **most innovation is bringing a new or incremental level of value** to your product offerings. So, you should be able to price for that, right? Or at least sell *less* for the *same* price.

There is another argument for this approach which oversimplifies the innovation process. If you can build whatever you want, why can't you just choose the ingredients, packaging, and size, etc. to create a higher margin than the established core offerings? The problem is, innovation usually starts with a *consumer-driven idea* – you can't just build whatever you want to. That consumer benefit we are trying to deliver will drive choices on key product attributes. So, if your innovation is about high fiber, that will cost more money than low fiber.

A third argument for accretive innovation is risk-based. If you launch something at a lower margin and it really takes off, it will pull down the margin of the whole business! Also, what if it doesn't take off? Usually, if sales are lower than expected, the margin drops even more! This leads to fear-based thinking: *There's so much risk involved, so let's protect the business and make it really worth our while.*

School of thought #2: Innovation is an investment, and the margin will increase with scale over time

This is often the perspective of innovation purists, who are primarily focused on driving growth. Their argument is that the base business will deliver margin, and the role of innovation is to bring new consumers into the business. It's an investment in long-term growth, no different than advertising or spending on sales promotions. So, it's okay if innovation launches with a lower margin, especially at first.

The most heated part of this argument usually centers around a desire from innovators to **deliver a high-quality product that meets or exceeds consumers' expectations.** A lot of innovations have an ideal benefit in mind in the idea phase. Once the team reaches the development phase, they often find the cost of that benefit is high. The innovation purist will throw their hands up and say, "Well, that's the cost of delivering what consumers want!"

Proponents of this argument will also point out that innovations start from nothing, so in their first year or two they are usually much smaller in scale than the base business. How can you expect something new and small in scale to have the same manufacturing costs as those established products that run so smoothly? **As innovation scales, the margin typically improves.** You find ways to speed up the manufacturing with experience, and you get cost breaks for higher volume. So, why set super-high targets at launch?

These schools of thought on innovation financials might sound like they're opposites, but I agree with both. Yes, margin should be accretive, *and* innovation needs room to build scale over time.

Let's start with why margins should be accretive. There are two things about decretive innovation that I've learned the hard way.

1. **If you launch margin-decretive innovation, even if it succeeds and sticks in market, companies will still often decide to discontinue it a few years later.** Why? Manufacturing teams are usually given cost savings targets every year, so they are constantly evaluating which of the products they run are the most efficient. Low-margin items, especially if they are also smaller from a volume perspective, will show up as savings opportunities. Your product will be first in line to be cut.

2. **Decretive innovation rarely gets long-term support from marketing.** You simply CANNOT AFFORD to keep investing in advertising on a low-margin part of the business. Sure, in year one, the innovation is losing money anyway. But on an ongoing basis, it will have a fully loaded P&L and will need to be able to make operating profit dollars *after* all the investment is behind it.

It's sounding an awful lot like I'm picking School of Thought #1, isn't it? But there's some nuance to my perspective. I think margin has to be evaluated *holistically,* at the portfolio level, not just project by project. And this allows for individual projects to have lower margins.

So, the margin target for innovation should be either:

1. parity to the <u>company average</u> margin, not the specific product line average, or

2. decretive to the business, at a level that will NOT reduce the overall business margin.

So, the next step is setting an appropriate decretive margin target for innovation.

Setting an appropriate decretive margin target provides a balanced approach. It allows for some initial investment in the innovation to deliver a high-quality product that will attract new users. It also accounts for the fact that innovations, if successful, tend to increase in margin over time. Nothing is more frustrating as an innovator than realizing, a year after launch, that you priced higher than you needed to and now your margin is well above your internal average. That's because it likely means you left revenue (growth) on the table, assuming a lower price would have generated a higher velocity of sales.

So, how do you set the *right* target?

Essentially you must **create a formula that sets different targets for different types of innovation projects.** You should assume that smaller innovation, being closer to your standard offerings, can easily achieve parity or accretive margins. Bigger innovation, on the other hand, is more complex and costly and needs some margin forgiveness. Here's a simple five-step process to help you (there's an example below, so you can see how these steps come to life):

- **Step 1:** Create a simple chart, like the one below, that calculates profit from sales and margin inputs and then adds those to calculate a total business margin.

- **Step 2:** With help from finance, input your base business sales and current average margin into the chart.

- **Step 3:** Estimate the percentage of your business you expect each type of innovation to be (likely a small percentage of the total). You can base this on historical innovation performance or on the targets associated with your current pipeline.

- **Step 4:** Starting with your base business margin, adjust the margin target for each type of innovation; it should be highest for smaller launches and lowest for bigger launches.

- **Step 5:** Look at the impact these margins have on your total business margin, and keep adjusting the targets for innovation until the total margin <u>matches</u> your base business average margin.

Congrats! Now you've set appropriate decretive margin targets!

I recommend putting the effort required into this process. It will help to make innovation a financial success over time. It allows you to protect overall business margins (keeping the executives happy) while also giving big bet innovations the financial room they need to create truly unique offerings. It is a true win-win approach.

Whatever you decide, it's important to **set clear financial targets for innovation and stick to them.** When margin targets are known at the beginning of a project, a smart innovation team will figure out pricing and cost targets very early on. This allows development to happen within cost parameters; good guardrails keep creative feet on the ground.

ANALYSIS FOR SETTING A DECRETIVE MARGIN TARGET

FACTS:

- AVERAGE MARGIN FOR YOUR PRODUCT LINE = 30%
- % BUSINESS FROM INNOVATION LAUNCHED IN LAST 3 YEARS = 15%
- SPLIT OF VOLUME ACROSS SMALL, MEDIUM, BIG-BET INNOVATION IS 10%/2.5%/2.5%
- YOUR BUSINESS IS PROJECTED TO BE $1 MM IN SALES TOTAL

QUESTION FOR ANALYSIS:

85% OF YOUR BUSINESS WILL BE AT 30% MARGIN, WHAT IS THE LOWEST % THE INNOVATION CAN BE AT BEFORE THE 30% MARGIN DROPS?

- YOU'LL WANT TO SET DIFFERENT TARGETS FOR SMALL, MEDIUM AND BIG BET INNOVATION.
- SO THIS ANALYSIS WILL BE COMPLEX. YOU'LL NEED HELP FROM YOUR FINANCE TEAM.
- I RECOMMEND SETTING SMALL INNOVATION TARGET AT ACCRETIVE, OR HIGHER, BECAUSE YOU CAN OFTEN EASILY HIT THIS ON THE CLOSER-IN PROJECTS.

EXAMPLE ANSWER

	BASE BUSINESS	SMALL INNOVATION	MEDIUM INNOVATION	BIG BET INNOVATION	TOTAL PROFIT	MARGIN %
% BUSINESS	85%	10%	2.5%	2.5%		
$ SALES	$850,000	$100,000	$25,000	$25,000		
MARGIN TARGETS	30%	32%	27%	25%		
RESULTING PROFIT	$255,000	$32,000	$6,750	$6,250	$300,000	30.0%

THE MARGINS MUST MATCH!

Without this clarity of approach, you may find your innovators holding a gun to the head of management at the end of a project, asking them to accept severely decretive launches. You may also need to cancel innovation after significant development work (read: resource usage) has already taken place.

And, best of all, when your innovation is incredibly needy but adorably profitable post-launch, no one will wonder if they should send your little tyrant to a shelter (I would never!).

CHAPTER FIVE

LET'S STOP LYING ABOUT OUR INNOVATION FORECASTS

I've probably touched close to a thousand food and beverage innovation projects in my career, across categories, channels, and companies. For some strange reason, I would say at least a quarter of those were initially forecasted at the exact same revenue: $20 million. Even weirder, that number hasn't changed over the past 25 years. Hmmmm.

For a few years, I led a team where manufacturing required a minimum innovation size of 1 million pounds of volume. I started noticing a pattern. About 90% of the projects my team submitted had a forecast of ... exactly 1 million pounds of product. What on earth?

Here's a dirty little secret: *Innovators lie* **about their revenue forecasts.**

Why do innovators lie about their forecasts? Innovators are the ones held accountable when the numbers don't come in as planned. They get called in front of management to explain the results. So, wouldn't it be self-defeating to lie? Maybe. But we do.

There are two main reasons we lie about our forecasts:

1. **It's really hard to generate an accurate innovation forecast.** There's never a perfect in-market item to compare your product to, and building a bottom-up forecast requires a lot of analytics. If instead of building a forecast yourself you opt for innovation forecasting research, if will likely come at a high cost. Worse, the leading innovation forecasting companies are not viewed as reliable and accurate by a lot of executives.

2. **We want to get our projects approved, and higher numbers make that more likely.** Executives want to believe a high level of growth is possible, and they often set unrealistic expectations, saying "think bigger" in response to forecasts they aren't excited by. Often, no one questions the logic behind the numbers if they are big enough, and this lack of pushback breeds laziness in innovation forecasts. Indeed, innovators will often pick the exact minimum forecast required for approval. Exaggerating a project's potential is better than having it canceled, especially when there are so many other ways to fail.

Understandable, you might think.

The problem is, lying about an innovation forecast will drive long-term failure.

I always think about innovation like a three-legged stool. One leg is the strength of the idea, one leg is the strength of the product, and the final leg is the strength of the execution in market from marketing and sales. If you kick one of the legs out, the stool topples. If you say an innovation will produce a high revenue and then it underdelivers, even if the product has still done well in the market, the project is viewed *internally* as a failure, and marketing and sales won't want to support it anymore. Once leadership decides it isn't working, you won't be able to get the support you need to make that innovation's long-term success a priority.

That's important and worth restating:

> **Even if an innovation is viewed *externally* as a success, if it's viewed as a failure *internally* because it missed its forecast, it will fail over the long term.**

Let's look at that in more detail. What actually happens if you miss your internal forecast? You will have veered away from your business case. Probably not just on revenue either; costs often rely on scale, so a lower revenue result can drive costs up and margin down. And if this innovation was key to your growth as a business, you are probably undermining your business's annual plan too. Now cost cutting will be required in order to deliver your annual profit goal. Where are the cuts likely to come from? Your sales and marketing support for the innovation that's underdelivering. Wow, that all went south really fast.

I've seen innovations that brought in over $50 million in *year one* that were still considered huge failures internally because they didn't perform as promised in the forecast.

Now we understand why it happens and just how damaging it can be. So, let's stop lying and do the work to create a *good* forecast.

But how do we forecast innovation accurately?

There are three fundamental models: trial and repeat, quartile analysis, and distribution and velocity (see the illustration in a few pages called "Innovation Forecasting Methods" for the calculations required for each).

1. **Trial and repeat forecast.** This is based on simple math around how many people will buy your product initially (triers) and how many will come back and buy it again (repeaters). Since most companies don't have a huge database of trial and repeat results, it's far too easy to justify high numbers and an unrealistic forecast using this method alone.

    I call this "marketing math," and it's my least favorite forecasting conversation. It usually goes something like this: "So … there are 300 million households in the U.S.; it's reasonable to assume 5% of them will try us. …" These superficial assumptions are typically not backed up by research or analytics.

    You can avoid this trap by using a marketing research company to build a trial and repeat forecast for you. With a larger database of comparable launches and consumer feedback, they can build a more comprehensive picture; but this can be expensive and time-consuming to do right.

    The final challenge with trial and repeat models? How long it will take to find out whether your forecast is on track. Trial and repeat really shouldn't be read in market until several purchase cycles have passed. In other words, you should wait until people have bought items in your category multiple times after launch, giving them multiple chances to buy *your* innovation. For a lot of product categories, that means you can't accurately measure trial and repeat for six months or even a year.

2. **Quartile analysis forecast.** Quartile analysis builds a forecast based on typical sales rates in your category. To create this forecast, you begin by ranking all of the products in your category based on their sales. Break your list into four equal

groups: quartiles A through D, with D representing the lowest sales. Then pick mid-range (quartile B and C), comparable products as your best estimate for your innovation's sales. If you have this competitive data and several of the competitive products are similar to your innovation, this is the fastest way to produce a reasonable forecast.

This is a good approach as it counters our natural optimism about the potential of innovation. The "watch out" here is that we (lying innovators) often ignore that our base branded products are in lower quartiles than we would like and believe that the unique attributes of our innovations will make them float up to unrealistic levels of sales in the higher quartiles. The truth is, innovation will almost *never* be in quartile A in year one, as A is made up of the biggest items in your category. Quartiles B and C are much more likely positions, and if most of your base business is in D, there's a good possibility your innovation will be as well. Look at the products in each quartile, and pick realistic comparisons.

If you're creating a new category or your innovation product is very unique, it might be best to use a different method. Quartile analysis assumes your innovation will behave similarly to what is in market already.

3. **Distribution and velocity forecast.** This model looks at all your possible points of sale and how many units you will likely sell in each, building the forecast that way. So, for a snack product, you might be sold in grocery stores, mass stores, and convenience stores. To create a forecast for this snack product, you'll need to know what percentage of those stores you'll get distribution in as well as how many units you will sell for each point of distribution (your velocity) and how much you'll be

charging per unit (your price). Then you multiply all of those together to find out your sales. This is simple math, but it's hard to do accurately because it requires a solid analysis of your category to ensure your distribution, velocity, and pricing assumptions are valid.

This is my recommended and preferred method because it is the easiest to track against, since distribution and sales rate are readily available if you are buying scanner data in your company. That means a distribution and velocity forecast is also the easiest to adjust if you aren't hitting your forecast once you are in market with your innovation.

Use the illustration opposite to calculate each type of forecast.

INNOVATION FORECASTING METHODS

TRIAL & REPEAT

TRIAL % X NUMBER OF AVAILABLE HOUSEHOLDS

REPEAT % X NUMBER OF AVAILABLE HOUSEHOLDS

AVERAGE ANNUAL PURCHASED UNITS PER HH

DOLLARS PER UNIT

PROS/CONS

🙂 IF BASED ON MARKETING RESEARCH (DETAILED MODEL WITH BENCHMARKS), THEN CAN BE EFFECTIVE

😐 FORECASTING RESEARCH IS EXPENSIVE

☹️ HARD TO TRACK AT LAUNCH

☹️ SUBJECT TO "MARKETING MATH" WITH TOO HIGH ASSUMPTIONS ACROSS ALL 3 MEASURES (NEEDS TO BE BASED ON ACTUAL IN-MARKET RESULTS)

QUARTILE ANALYSIS

1. RANK ORDER ALL ITEMS IN YOUR CATEGORY BY THEIR ANNUAL REVENUE

2. DIVIDE INTO 4 QUARTILES - ABCD (A BEING THE HIGHEST)

3. LOOK AT B AND C QUARTILES (MAYBE EVEN D) AND PICK THE CLOSEST COMPARISONS FOR YOUR ITEM

PROS/CONS

🙂 BASED ON YOUR CATEGORY, SO ASSUMPTIONS ARE REALISTIC

😐 CAN FEEL PRESSURE TO PICK TOO HIGH OF A QUARTILE, RESULTING IN UNREALISTIC FORECAST

☹️ WON'T WORK IF YOU ARE CREATING A NEW CATEGORY OR IF YOUR ITEM IS VERY UNIQUE (PRICE PREMIUM TO EVERYTHING ELSE, FOR EXAMPLE)

DISTRIBUTION & VELOCITY

DISTRIBUTION (EXAMPLES: % ACV IF SOLD IN RETAIL, # STORES)

X

VELOCITY (EXAMPLE: UNITS SOLD PER % ACV OR STORE)

X

AVERAGE # UNITS PER PURCHASE

X

DOLLAR PRICE PER UNIT

PROS/CONS

🙂 MOST LIKELY TO BE ACCURATE

🙂 ASSUMPTIONS YOU CAN QUICKLY TRACK AT LAUNCH

☹️ TAKES A LOT OF TIME & ANALYSIS TO DO PROPERLY

YOU SHOULD BUILD SEPARATE DISTRIBUTION AND VELOCITY MODELS FOR EVERY CHANNEL OF BUSINESS AND THEN ADD THEM TOGETHER

A word about cannibalization.

All of the models we just discussed will calculate the total – or gross – predicted sales of an innovation. But innovations are almost never 100% incremental to a business, meaning they will likely steal from the sales of your existing offerings. In other words, there will be some cannibalization (the percentage of your innovation's sales that come from customers switching from your other products to this new item). And you'll need to understand this impact in order to fully build out your P&L.

Cannibalization is one of the trickiest innovation metrics to both predict and measure. I find it helpful to do an analysis of how incremental your own small, medium, and big bet innovations have been in the past and use this to create rules of thumb for cannibalization in your business. If you have a sharp analytics team, they can estimate this. If not, you can engage help from a research firm to estimate it by looking at shoppers' baskets before and after an innovation launch. Cannibalization will be highest for small innovations because they are usually most similar to what is already on the market; it should be lowest for big bet innovations because they are usually the most unique and most likely to address category barriers, which will draw new consumers into your business.

The good news is, because cannibalization is an inexact science, once you've looked at some historical data or done an analysis with a research firm, you can establish benchmark average cannibalization rates for small, medium, and big bets and stick to them when you build your plans. It's best to lock these assumptions down; otherwise, cannibalization will become another thing your innovators will lie about to make their P&L look better. :)

So, now we know how to create a better innovation forecast on an ad hoc basis. But do you want to allow all the innovators on your team the freedom to create forecasts their own way?

For long-term success and consistency in forecasting, it's worth going a step further and putting tools and processes in place that support the entire innovation team.

Below, I've outlined three that can have a big impact. These will dramatically increase the accuracy of your forecasts and your ability to react when an innovation gets off to a slow start. Put these in place as part of your successful innovation engine to create a disciplined forecasting approach.

1. **Have an analytics expert build a <u>forecast modeling tool</u> that everyone can use.**
   - Typically built in Excel, this model allows innovators to input assumptions and get a forecast spit out instantly.
   - Remember, do *not* build this using the trial and repeat model unless you have a lot of available internal comparison data.
   - Instead, build this model using the distribution and velocity model, with separate tabs in the Excel file for each channel of business you compete in and then a summary tab that adds all of those individual channel forecasts up.
   - The forecasting tool should include helpful comparisons, like the past few years of innovations in your category and how they have performed on each of these metrics.
   - Base business comparisons can also be included, but these can be problematic. Innovation forecasts should *not* assume they can achieve metrics similar to the base business, especially not in year one. Innovation will not perform like the top items in the base portfolio out of the gate. Assume you will perform more like your mid-tier items.
   - **Pro tip:** Build the quartile analysis method into the tool to

avoid this trap. Provide a rank ordering of all of the items in the category based on their distribution and velocity. Your tool can even show what the average distribution or velocity rate is for a C quartile item in your category as a default suggestion!

2. **Schedule a regular <u>innovation forecast approval meeting</u>.**
   - However, don't make this in-depth discussion of forecasting part of your existing stage-gate meetings (where senior leaders approve innovations to move on to the next stage in their journey). I don't recommend this for two reasons:
     1. Forecast review is too detailed for most senior decision-makers. They are time poor and likely too far removed from the data to know how good the assumptions are.
     2. You don't need all of your stage-gate decision-makers in a forecast approval meeting, so you'll be wasting a lot of folks' time.
   - A forecast approval meeting should include representatives from sales, marketing, analytics, consumer insights, and whoever your final decision-maker is on forecasts. You may also want to include someone from finance, since the forecast will be a key P&L input.
   - In the meeting, the innovator should review each of the main assumptions – distribution, velocity, price, and cannibalization – with the intent of ensuring all the commercial stakeholders are aligned. If the forecast is big, the innovator should probably talk to some of the attendees in advance in order to double-check their assumptions (especially sales!). But this meeting will ensure that conversation happens if it has not already.
   - **It's worth mentioning that this meeting can help prevent the knee-jerk reaction from executives that something "should be bigger."** The tool is just math, so if everyone agrees the

assumptions are valid, then they should agree the forecast is right. If executives want it to be bigger, they have to change the inputs. Can sales commit to more distribution? Is there enough marketing support to convince us this will outperform other innovation launches in our category on velocity? Can we price higher? If not, they need to trust the analysis.

- I recommend holding this meeting monthly and reviewing all projects that have either just started or are about to launch. Keep in mind that there will be *lots* of iterations of innovation forecasts throughout the life of a bigger project, but a formal review of the first forecast created and the last one used to lock in the financials is critical.

3. **Build an <u>innovation forecast tracker</u> in the months before an innovation launches that will allow you to quickly see if your projects are behind.**
    - Sales should create a distribution tracker by customer, with how many stores or distribution slots are expected and how many have been confirmed.
    - An analytics expert should help build a forecast of how velocity will grow over time. Unless they have *huge* marketing support on day one, innovations usually grow to their final turn rate over one to two years. But tracking whether your velocity is increasing as expected is important.
    - Once you have these tracking elements in place, schedule a regular review of them as early as four weeks into launch with marketing, sales, and analytics. Why? Because the earlier you notice that your innovation is behind, the more likely you are to get internal support to FIX rather than ABANDON the innovation.

Even with solid innovation forecasting discipline in place, innovation is still unpredictable. The market might change on you (making the comparisons you used invalid), or the competition might launch something similar, eating into your trial. I could go on – unfortunately, as we know, the ways to fail are numerous.

But having the most accurate forecast up front will give your innovation its best chance. It will maximize the internal support you receive when your new item is in market and it'll help you to keep track of whether it's delivering on expectations. **In an uncertain environment, it's better to be smart than lucky.**

And don't worry, innovators. There's still plenty of other aspects of innovation we can lie about, like our timelines! *evil laugh*

— *SNACK BREAK* —

ARE YOU OUT HERE SPLITTING TRIAL LIKE A <u>DUMBO</u>?

Trial matters.

I just told you in the last chapter not to use predictions of trial purchases in your forecasting. And I meant it. I wouldn't.

But the percentage of people who try your innovation in year one is probably the single most predictive metric of innovation success. If it weren't so hard to both predict and measure, we would all focus on trial way more. You want trial rates to be as high as possible. It will drive your sales velocity (the number of units per point of distribution you sell).

But there's one mistake that innovators often make that undermines their trial rates. A common approach to innovation is to launch three to four new items as a product "line." I don't know why so many of us have that paradigm in our heads, but we do – indeed, it's something I've done several times over the years. But it's problematic.

When you launch two, three, or four new items that all have the same new core benefit but just come in different scents, sizes, flavors, or colors, **you *split* your trial purchases.** I'll explain what I mean by that. Your consumers only buy a certain amount of products in your category every year. Innovation rarely manages to be much more than 10 or 20% incremental to the total category, meaning it usually doesn't make people use *more* soap or eat *more* cookies – they continue to use the same amount. If they look at a lot of items with a similar benefit, they will narrow down their choice to the acceptable range of products that meet their needs and then switch between those. In other words, you only have a limited number of purchases to play with.

Because your consumers will just pick *one* from the two, three, or four varieties you've launched, the more similar innovation items you offer at once, the more you are cannibalizing your own products, and the more likely the trial purchases of each will be smaller. In other words, you are splitting your trial up among multiple items.

When this happens, small innovations get declared a failure. You could theoretically launch a line that's on forecast, and really big in total, but where each variety is in the C or D quartile and at risk of being discontinued. It may be discontinued by your internal manufacturing or sales teams, who see the sales are small and inefficient for them, or by your customers or distribution partners, who don't think the sales justify their warehouse or shelf space.

I have done this exact thing, multiple times. I shot my innovation in the foot.

Innovators, please: Think about how much variety your innovation actually needs. One item might get lost in the sea of choices on the shelf, so yes, maybe you do need two. But do you really need three or four? Think carefully.

Okay, rant over. Have these last few chapters been too business-booky? Don't emergency exit yet!! Let's talk about creativity next.

CHAPTER SIX

POPPING CANDY AND BREAKFAST PIZZA? CREATIVITY ISN'T ABOUT BEING WEIRD

Think of the *most creative innovation* your broader category has ever launched (seriously, just stop for a second and think of one).

Was it truly successful? *Or was it just newsworthy?*

Unfortunately, as humans, when we think of "creative" products, a lot of the time we just think of weird stuff. Every time I've ever hosted a food ideation session, people think of the same weird things over and over again. Using Pop Rocks® (the most popular U.S. brand of popping candy) as an ingredient or topping has been suggested in at least 90% of them. For the record, that is NOT a good idea ... sorry popping candy, but you are best eaten alone. The other weird thing people want to do? Turn everything into a toaster pastry or a pizza. Breakfast pizza. Salad pizza. Dessert pizza. Apparently, pizza = creative in our minds. I'm not sure why, but it's true (and, trust me on this, weird pizza innovations will test well but fail in market).

NOT ALL
WEIRD PIZZA IS GOOD

You might also think of those brown sodas that were launched with new "clear" versions or potato chips with strange flavors like roast chicken or crab. And what about the DeLorean® in automobiles?

In reality, the best ideas are not weird ... they're *obvious*.

And by obvious, I mean they address well-known consumer concerns. They're not trying to create something you've never seen before. Successful innovation is usually practical. It makes the consumer experience easier and quicker and less stressful. Here's some great innovations that grew their categories: Land O'Lakes® Half Butter Sticks, Crisco® Spray, Quaker® Instant Oatmeal, and Tide® Pods.

What do they all have in common? They solved problems for consumers. Simple as that. Crayola® didn't invent crayons; they just made them accessible and safe for children (previously, they were a toxic and expensive adult art supply).

The best innovations also often take a product people are already familiar with and make it more user-friendly or convenient. They solve the things people *hate* about the category or brand. And, before you object, even consumers that *love* you will have things they *hate* about you. Brands are just like people; they aren't perfect. In fact, I've found that the best innovation ideas have usually been around for *years*, meaning the leading brands in the category have known this consumer problem existed for a long time and have been unsuccessful in their attempts to solve it. Every marketer you meet who worked at Kraft® in the 00s will tell you they invented EasyMac®, a microwavable mac and cheese cup. I suspect that's because Kraft worked on EasyMac for so long that multiple waves of employees feel like it was their success! It was a simple way to make mac and cheese even more convenient to make.

I like to joke that **there are no new ideas, only new people.** What I mean is that lots of people will go through a company over time, and they'll probably all suggest the same innovation solutions because they're trying to solve the same problems. It's often those who understand the business, brand, and category best who have the clearest grasp of the "obvious" innovation ideas. I try to shortcut this process when I first join a new business. I ask the technical developers, "What have you been trying to figure out forever and haven't cracked?"

However, I want to make one thing clear: By "obvious" I don't mean "copycat."

Often, people who are new to a business (or misguided executives) will say, "Hey, our competitor is making boatloads of money with

XYZ. We should make our own version!" This may seem "obvious" to them, but it's amateur hour.

Copycat innovations almost always fail unless one of the following things is true:
1. They launch immediately after a competitor's version does or during a big trend (see the Greek yogurt and spiked seltzer innovation storms).
2. Your brand has significantly more power and scale than the originating brand (so a lot of consumers will think it was your idea because they didn't hear about the other one).
3. They are much better quality (noticeably ... and to real people, not experts) than the original (this is rare).

The only other exception to this rule is 4. cheaper private label or value brand offerings which *intend* to be copycat (the store brand version, for example). If that's your business model, ignore this (and also, I'm sorry, but your innovation job is boring). I bring up copycats here because *really bad* copycat innovation ideas will come up over and over again. Remember that good ideas solve a *consumer* problem. Copying something solves *your* problem as a business (you wishing you had that money your competitor is making from their idea).

Once you've got that great idea, the real creativity begins – execution!

You've finally landed on this big, obvious idea that will make consumers love your category more. It hasn't yet launched because it's hard or expensive to solve – or, even more likely, both hard *and* expensive. If you can solve the roadblocks around capital, packaging, pricing, financials, or communication clarity, you'll have a hit on your hands. Creativity comes to the forefront here in finding the solution to getting this innovation to market.

This is why some of the best leaders in innovation are both creative *and* practical. There are those who just want to think about the big ideas, and *not* how to make them happen. They're untethered to reality, thinking of "creativity" as something separate from everyday life. The best innovators understand that the idea is only the starting point. Rather than flitting from one idea to another whenever they meet resistance, they stick with the big idea and keep pivoting to find creative solutions that make it work.

So, how do you solve the seemingly unsolvable problems that are stopping your big innovation ideas getting to market? I find the best way to do that is to understand the root of the issue and try to reframe the problem.

- *The packaging is just too expensive!* Can you pack it a different way?
- *The capital is too high to pay back!* What else could you make with that capital? Can you bundle two initiatives to justify it? Can you launch it on a smaller scale to prove the financials out? Can you find a contract manufacturer to share the investment with?
- *The margins are too low!* Can you get creative on the sizing to reduce costs? Can you add premium features that allow for an increase in price?

If you can find the solution, you may still have an uphill battle convincing the organization to take a run at an idea they have tried before. It is important to focus *equally* on why the idea is still right for the consumer, *and* how you are changing the project to make your chance at success much higher this time.

But what if you *don't* have that great idea?

Okay, so let's say you DON'T have one of these obvious ideas to chase. You've read this whole chapter thinking, *What is she talking about?* Or perhaps there is one, but only one, and you need to fill your pipeline with more than just a single home run. How do you get creative without getting ... weird? Simple. **Have very clear creative guardrails.**

Whenever I say creativity needs guardrails in a brainstorming session, I often get the same pushback from inexperienced innovators: "Isn't creativity about being open-minded? Why do you want to *put us in a box*?" My favorite way to answer that is to get them to do an exercise.

Think of every word that you know. Set a timer for three minutes, and write them down. *(Seriously, stop reading for a second and try it.)*

When people try to do this, they usually start by writing down either what they are thinking about in that moment or what they see right in front of them. Then, about a minute in, when that thought process runs dry, they come up with a system. There's usually some variation in approach from person to person. Someone might pick a letter of the alphabet and write down all the words that start with that letter. I also often see people doing word association exercises that essentially result in them writing down all the words associated with a category – like every animal they can think of.

This exercise shows us that in the absence of guardrails, humans invent them. Why? *Because it's easier to be creative with some guardrails.*

Sometimes, after they've completed the exercise, I'll set another three-minute timer and say, "Now write down every word you can think of associated with school." Usually, with tighter guardrails, people come up with far more words.

Someone recently gave me an analogy for this that really stuck. If you are crossing a one-lane bridge, she said, you will drive *a lot* faster if there are guardrails because you'll be less scared. I love that.

So, how do you set innovation guardrails? Well, I explain this in detail in Chapter Thirteen, which is on innovation strategies. For now, I'll just hit the highlights.

You can set innovation guardrails by answering three questions:
1. What are the *critical elements* of this brand/product line that I need to maintain? What is critical to my brand's competitive positioning?
2. What are the elements we are open to changing?
3. Are there specific new product or packaging technologies or benefits we desire?

When you answer these questions, think *broadly*. Consider the usage occasion, product form, packaging form, packaging size, product attributes (shape, size, appearance, benefit, value), ingredients, and selling location (channel, part of store). Write these guardrails down, and open any brainstorm by sharing them.

Guardrails make us more creative, not less – our ideas just become smarter and more targeted. So, try thinking INSIDE the box for once (just remember to cut some breathing holes).

And, please, do yourself a favor and don't bring up popping candy or breakfast pizza in the brainstorm.

— *SNACK BREAK* —

NO PIZZA FOR YOU!

If you just read that chapter about creativity and now you're thinking about what weird pizzas you could make, take a break and get some fresh air. And don't, under any circumstances, say that innovation sounds like fun.

I MEAN IT!

PART II:

THE "FUN" PART

HOW TO HARNESS CREATIVITY IN INNOVATION

— *MENTAL BREAK* —

Hang on a minute ... a *whole* SECTION about FUN??

How DARE I!

But don't worry. You'll see I wrote "fun" in quotes, with a side of sarcasm. That's because people *think* front-end innovation work is fun ... including most innovators. But we've had this conversation before. We might love this work, but it's often a grueling uphill battle.

In case you've forgotten, innovation is *ugly*.

— SNACK BREAK —

IF YOU DON'T HAVE A BEST FRIEND IN INSIGHTS, YOU AREN'T DOING IT RIGHT

I recently had to complete one of those get-to-know-you surveys for a newsletter, and one of the questions was, "What three words would your best friend use to describe you?" I texted her for an answer. She replied: "Creative. Witty. Red."

She gets me. Red is my favorite color. I overuse it in both my wardrobe and presentations as a result. It's also the color I turn when excited, sad, mad, embarrassed, outside, drinking … you get the point; I flush easily. Red: It's a pretty good word to describe me.

My best friend works in consumer insights. It's fair to say her job is to figure people out. Then she explains them to innovators and executives. She does that on a large scale, leveraging research and analytics to do so. Insights are *critical* to the success of innovation because innovation **has to start and end with a consumer need.** The job of the innovator is to shepherd the innovation project through development *without losing sight* of that consumer need.

If you do lose sight of that need (which is much easier than you think), you will compromise the purity of the concept and launch something that's feasible for your company but that may not make a difference to the people buying it. As an innovator, consumer insights people are your conscience. They are the talking cricket on your shoulder that constantly reminds you why you are doing what you're doing. They'll steer you toward what is right for the consumer … and warn you what is just a selfish choice for the business.

Whether you're a marketer, a project manager, or an R&D professional, you need to be close friends with your insights partner if you want your innovation to be successful. In fact, I would argue that no matter what your role is in innovation, this is probably true. And I've emphasized the importance of insights so much at home that my daughter became an insights professional.

So, now I have *two* best friends in insights, which makes me really happy. Happy slash red.

CHAPTER SEVEN

WHAT THE DUCK DO YOU OWN? (POINTS OF DIFFERENCE)

I've worked on a lot of failed innovations in my career. Look, innovation is ugly (have I already said that?). And I've spent a lot of time thinking about WHY they either failed to launch ... failed at launch ... or just plain failed in market. Over time, I noticed a common theme around their point of difference (what sets them apart from the competition).

In many cases, innovations that failed didn't have a point of difference that was *consumer-driven and meaningful, ownable*, and *single-minded*.

It turns out this matters. A lot. These three phrases are critical (and a mouthful), so let's look at them in more detail.

1. CONSUMER-DRIVEN AND MEANINGFUL

Any point of difference (POD) at all can help you stand out and gain share if you shout it. Quick, think of an annoying radio or TV ad you hear all the time. I bet you can tell me their POD off the top of your head (do they have the "best internet bundle" around?). These PODs might be memorable, but are they meaningful?

To thrive in the long term, you need to do more than break through the noise of the marketplace. You need to think about your *consumer* and not just your competition. Meaningful PODs matter to them. I might have the only blue widget in my category. That's a POD. But does the color of the widget matter to the consumer? Are people just as happy with an orange widget?

In order to know if your POD matters, you either need to know your target consumer really well (maybe through your best friend in insights?) or you need to ask consumers what matters most to them. If you ask them, be careful of what I call the "coolest minivan" effect. If you ask consumers to look at a list of minivans and tell you which one is the coolest, they will pick one. But that top-ranked minivan will still not be cool because minivans are *not cool* (sorry, suburban families everywhere). The same thing can happen with innovation benefits. If you have consumers pick from a shortlist of choices that you've decided on, it may be that none of those are meaningful to them, and you may pick a POD or idea that doesn't address a consumer need. Instead, you must do this work at the beginning, as part of your strategic foundation, to understand what your consumer is looking for. We'll talk even more about that when we discuss strategy in Chapter Thirteen.

If you are innovating on a really strong brand built around its unique benefit versus competition, it's possible that your innovation's POD will be the same as the overall brand's. Make sure that point of difference remains relevant; if it's outdated, you may be better served stretching your brand in a new direction rather than relying on its current equity.

One last warning on this topic. I can think of two major innovations I worked on that failed within a year because we launched with a POD that wasn't meaningful to *our* consumer. It was meaningful to a consumer we *aspired* to have, but not the one we actually had. So, when you're working on something as fundamental as an innovation POD, concentrate on the hard data about the people who actually buy your product. Talk to them.

2. OWNABLE

It's not enough to have a meaningful, consumer-driven idea; it also has to be ownable. This should be clear, given that all of these adjectives we are stepping through are modifying the phrase "point of difference." If your benefit isn't unique in your category, your innovation is a copycat. Remember what I said about copycats in Chapter Six?

The problem is that most ideas are *not* ownable because they aren't truly unique. What's your point of difference for your current lead project? If the answer is something like convenience, taste, fun, value, or a category-generic benefit like cleaning power, your innovation probably isn't that different from a lot of existing offerings in your category.

A true point of difference is something that NO ONE else is doing. This is hard to achieve in a base business because open competition tends to bring big brands closer together in any given category. But innovation provides that opportunity. It can bring something entirely new to a category, and that can be really powerful. If you are the only one with a meaningful, consumer-driven benefit, you are going to win tons of consumers over to your business.

One of the risks around ownability comes when you do trend-forward innovation. If everyone is talking about something, everyone is probably working on it too. You will think your competition "stole" your idea, but in reality, they just saw the same trends as you and responded to them. If you have a major launch relying on a trend, think about what would happen if the other brands in your category launched first or at the same time as you. Would you still succeed? One of my biggest, most expensive failures happened because the bigger brand beat us to market with our extremely meaningful point of difference, and it was therefore no longer ownable.

3. SINGLE-MINDED

Finally, successful innovation PODs are single-minded. By that, I mean that there's one, simple takeaway for consumers. It's the short, straightforward message you can point to in your advertising. You should be able to explain it in three words or less on the front of the packaging in the store or on the website. *It's smaller. It's easier. It's faster. It's cheaper. It's sexier.* (Not all of those at once though!)

In my experience, innovations with multiple points of difference – it's fun and fast and good value – never work. It's too hard to fit that on the package or in the ad, meaning it also won't fit into a consumer's brain.

In fact, the more crowded your market is with competitive brands, the more single-minded your POD should be. Otherwise, it'll never stand out from the crowd or be memorable.

This reminds me of those theories on sibling rivalry. As a parent myself, I love talking about this. When you have one child, you will see them as complex and "their own person." When you have two, you will end up with a "good kid" and a "bad kid" (if you are one of two and don't agree with this, you are probably the bad kid. Sorry!). Once you have three or more, it's much harder for any one child to stand out. They are competing for a dwindling share of their parents' attention, in the same way we all compete for our consumers' attention in a busy marketplace. Unconsciously, kids will find unique and ownable points of difference in order to get the attention they desire. When you have *seven* kids, like my parents did, those PODs become *very* single-minded. There's the bossy one, the goody-two-shoes, the rebel, the football-head, etc. One-note personalities. (I, of course, was the bossy one as the responsible oldest child.) If you are in a crowded space, you have to simplify to stand out.

So, if you want to keep failure at bay, evaluate your ideas' PODs across these filters early on, and if they don't hit the mark, be brutal in moving on.

✓ CONSUMER-DRIVEN AND MEANINGFUL

✓ OWNABLE

✓ SINGLE-MINDED

Yikes. This is a tough standard to reach, but it's probably the most highly correlated one to an innovation's success. As we know, there are so many ways to fail, so don't let this one trip you up. If your innovations pass the test, you'll be able to begin your project from a foundation of strength.

Side note: Autocorrect changed the headline of this chapter to "duck." You and I both know that's not what I wrote. I promised in the preface this book wouldn't be about AI, but man, some of it is still really ducking bad.

— *SNACK BREAK* —

HATE, HATE, HATE ... LOATHE ENTIRELY

The title of this snack break is a line from the 2000 movie *How the Grinch Stole Christmas*. The Grinch is talking about the people of Whoville; I say it all the time when I'm talking about innovation. And I'm not talking about how hard it is; I'm talking about the power of knowing what consumers *hate* about your category.

The best, most powerful innovation ideas fix a current problem with the category. But finding a consumer-driven, meaningful, ownable, single-minded innovation benefit can sometimes be easier said than done. In the last chapter, I showed how many ways your point of difference can fall apart. The truth is consumers aren't always conscious of how frustrating or inconvenient their experience with a product or service is. They just accept the realities of it. *Ice cream melts and makes a mess. Aluminum foil packaging cuts my fingers. Mortgage applications are confusing and hard. That's just the way it is* *shrug*. That's why it is practically impossible to ask consumers to ideate breakthrough innovation, unless you specifically screen for creative-minded people who can imagine new possibilities.

But.

I have found a way to get at true unmet needs through consumer research. And it's really simple. It's called hate research, and it really comes down to two simple steps:

1. **Talk to your category's EXTREME consumers (at both ends)**
    a. The heavy users (the LOVERS)
    b. The very light users or complete rejectors of your category (the HATERS)
2. **Ask them what they HATE about your category (even if the lovers mostly love it)**

Let's look at an example. We all *love* ice cream. First, list all the things you love about it (on your own). Great. With that out of the way, what do you *hate* about it? For example: Why does the carton collapse in the freezer and then the lid comes off because the carton is misshapen and then the ice cream gets freezer burn and then I have to scoop that frostbitten part out and put it down the sink? *deep breath*

When you start to push those two groups of consumers (lovers and haters) on what they hate, they will come through. After all, everyone loves a good rant. This works even better in a group, whether virtual or in person, because people will wind each other up.

Hate research turns up true unmet needs in your category – the problems that, if solved, will win you huge share and attract light users … and maybe even rejectors! That will make your innovation far more incremental to your existing business.

But what if it's impossible to ask people what they hate about your category?

For a variety of reasons, you can't always ask consumers this hate question. Perhaps it's a technical category and they can't articulate the true causes of the issues without specialist knowledge. Maybe the category has a lot of cliché or red herring problems that everyone knows about (like the fact ice cream melts and makes a mess) that get in the way of getting to deeper problems you could actually solve. Or perhaps you can't talk to your consumer like an adult because they're *kids*.

Many years ago, when I worked in toys, we wanted to create a remote control car that would compete with the amazing stuff the leading brand was launching at the time. We wanted it to have a new-to-the-world feature that would be really compelling for kids.

The problem was, we didn't have any good ideas about what that could be.

So, we asked parents to videotape their kids playing with their favorite remote control car. And then I watched *hours and hours* of footage (until my contacts literally peeled out of my eyes in a rejection of my life choices).

I looked for moments of frustration, and I found one that happened *a lot*. In ads, remote controlled cars are always shown tearing through a desert landscape, kicking up dust, and flying over mounds of dirt. In reality, kids almost always played with their cars in their driveways or apartment parking lots.

In that environment, the only really exciting landscape feature is the *street curb*. And the kids wanted their cars to fly right over it. But they didn't. When the cars were driven over the curb, they nosedived and landed on their backs like an upside-down turtle, wheels spinning in the air. When they were driven toward the curb, they crashed into it and came to a stop. When kids tried to make the cars climb up the curb, they failed and flopped over. In each of these scenarios, inevitably, the kids had to go and manually pick the car up and set it upright. Their body language would be so defeated and frustrated. Having to move your car around with your hand undermines the whole idea of *remote* control, doesn't it?

I spliced together key highlights from all the home video and showed it to our engineers. Could they make a remote control car that *jumped a curb* from either direction? Kids would *love* it. We did it, and it was the number-one-selling remote control car that holiday season – a huge accomplishment for a small player in the market.

So, if you can't *ask* what consumers hate about your category, **watch them use it and *observe* what frustrates them.**

Pay attention to people's workarounds.

If you're not getting enough feedback on the "hates," ask what your consumers do when a product doesn't work the way they want it to. Do they have to tip your package to get the product to come out of the nozzle? Do they need a knife to open it? Do they wrap it in plastic after it's open to keep it fresh? Do they need tape or clips or other materials to make it work the way it should? Do they place your product on a towel because it always makes a mess? Is it the right size for the occasion, or do they need to buy two to meet their needs? Is it *so* big that it doesn't fit on the shelf at home and has to be stored on top of the fridge? Or in the guest room? Or does it not fit in the fridge door, so they slide it in sideways on a shelf? If you can solve these little, everyday inconveniences, it can go a long way with consumers.

Make sure consumers want the problem to be solved.

A final warning. There will be aspects of a product consumers may complain about, but not really want fixed. Some of our favorite snacks are high in calories or sugar, but that doesn't mean we want healthier, lower-calorie, worse-tasting versions of them. The fact that they are sugary is *why* we crave them. This is why it's important to 1. get past the obvious "hates" for your category, to the deeper feelings or workarounds, and 2. test the ideas you identify to make sure people actually want them. Do *you* want ice cream that doesn't melt? Sounds suspicious.

Look carefully for the signs of frustration, identify the winning ideas, and learn to jump the curb.

CHAPTER EIGHT

DUMB BRAINSTORMS LEAD TO DUMB IDEAS

A bad brainstorm is worse than no brainstorm at all.

The *least effective* and *most common* is the "go, think, quick" brainstorm. It sounds like a Neanderthal is talking. And that should tell you everything you need to know.

Quick. Think of new ideas for chairs.

New kinds of chairs ... what do you got?

I'll let you write them down for the next 15 minutes; then we'll all share.

The problem is, this is *not* how humans are wired. Back in Chapter Six, we talked about how hard it is to be creative. How we all think of the same (dumb) ideas. But that often happens when we aren't *prepared* and we aren't *inspired*. Don't roll your eyes at me, executive; I'm being serious here. Inspiration matters.

When someone just says "go, think, quick" at us, we panic a little. Then typical human behavior drives us to think of 1. obvious things (a chair that is soft, so it doesn't hurt my butt), and 2. weird things (a chair that brings me pizza. Mmmm, pizza).

Dumb ideas come from dumb brainstorms. Don't waste everyone's time.

So, the real question is: How do I run an effective brainstorming session?

There are *nine key components* to making the most of these opportunities. I know. That's a lot. But if you do the work, you'll reap the rewards. (This chapter is a specific to-do list for brainstorms, designed for those with less innovation experience. If you are an expert, you can probably glance at the list below and skim through each component.)

1. Choose the right day and time
2. Use a good space or virtual tool
3. Select a strong brainstorm team
4. Have rules
5. Set clear guardrails
6. Create an agenda (with great ideation exercises)
7. Incorporate consumer learning
8. Provide a template to capture ideas
9. Have some freakin' fun!

So, let's start talking about how to do a brainstorm right.

1. CHOOSE THE RIGHT DAY AND TIME

Speaking from experience, people are more focused and creative on certain days of the week and at certain times of the day. I'm not going to explain all the science here; you can look it up online if you don't believe me.

The best *days* to host a brainstorm for corporate employees are just common sense: Tuesday or Wednesday. No one is focused on a Monday (they're too tired from staying up late on the weekend and too overwhelmed by everything that needs to happen that week). No one is focused on a Friday (they're too distracted thinking about the fact that the weekend is almost here and you are keeping them from it). And, if you didn't know, Thursday is the new Friday.

And the best *time* for a brainstorm is first thing in the morning. Morning people, rejoice (and then punch yourselves in the face, please). Even those of us who *feel* like we don't get started until 10 am are more focused first thing. I suspect it's why standardized testing happens early too.

DO NOT START A BRAINSTORM IN THE AFTERNOON (shouty all caps are required here; that's how strongly I feel). I don't care what the travel or scheduling challenges are. The only exception is if the afternoon is used as a prep session for a brainstorm that falls over multiple days. This will allow you to go over the guardrails and key learning to date before you kick off the actual brainstorming the next morning.

Our energy is lowest in the mid-afternoon. And you can't ask low-energy humans to be creative. I mean, you can, but they will probably just invent a chair that brings you pizza.

2. USE A GOOD SPACE OR VIRTUAL TOOL

When thinking about space, the first question is whether this brainstorm will be in person or virtual.

Virtual

If it's virtual, it's critical to find a tool that enables collaboration on ideas. There are a lot of online whiteboards with different brainstorming tools. You'll want something that allows people to create ideas that can be easily sorted, voted on, and dragged around. Whoever is moderating the session should be (or become) an expert at using this tool and be able to train the team on its basic functions in five minutes or less at the beginning of the brainstorm.

With a virtual whiteboard, I recommend setting up all of the exercises (see 5. The right agenda) you are going to do in advance, as sections of the whiteboard, with the instructions already typed in and some example ideas loaded as well.

In person

If you are doing a brainstorm in person, then one of the most important decisions you will make is the space.

Here are a few considerations:

- It needs to have a much higher capacity than the number of participants coming. Brainstorming requires moving around. The ability to get into small groups that are far enough apart from one another that they don't distract each other (and the ability to rearrange furniture for this purpose) is critical. There's something psychologically important about having *room* to think. Small spaces make people more uncomfortable, both physically and mentally. If you have 20 people attending, book a conference room for 50. If you're booking a room in your office, ask for the one used for big meetings and rearrange it for the brainstorm.

- Brainstorm spaces should have natural light; this brings in energy, whereas windowless rooms drain it. Ideally, it should also have a view. Looking over a landscape, especially one with green in it, is a great way to reset our brains.
- If the room doesn't have natural light, the colors in the room will be especially important. Think about calming blues and greens that don't distract your attendees. These shouldn't be too bright; I once had a brainstorm in a room with a wall that looked like it was painted to be a green screen – none of us could stand it!
- Seating should be chairs at tables. Don't go for "creative" rooms filled with armchairs or beanbag chairs or futons. Those signal "relaxation" to people. You may think it'll loosen them up, but they will actually switch off and come up with fewer ideas. Tables and chairs (like at school) signal it's time to work. Ideally, the tables should easily move around, so you can make different-sized groups throughout the day or have space to do some physical activities.

3. SELECT A STRONG BRAINSTORM TEAM

I personally think **the ideal brainstorm session has 15-20 people.** Not everyone agrees with me. Some ideation moderators will freak out and say that's too many. I do think 20 is the max; after that, the group is too hard to control.

I like 20ish because I want to be able to break into small teams of up to four people, and this allows for four or five groups, which is perfect. I also like to rotate who people partner with to ideate all day, and if you have a small number of attendees, that will be hard to do.

So, who should you invite?

Start with a broad internal team. Make sure you invite all the key functions that would work on the front end of an innovation project. This could include marketing, R&D, engineering, insights, analytics, and finance. It's important to include key technical experts in your company as they will know what is possible. They will also know which ideas have been around forever ... and they might be able to come up with a twist to make them (finally) work! Try to invite people you think are more open to possibilities vs. naysayers (but be aware that naysayers can become yes-people when the idea is theirs). And keep the energy-suckers away – the people who never have anything positive to say – if you can. That doesn't mean you should only invite your work friends or only extraverts as opposed to introverts (in my experience, the quiet team members can often be the strongest ideators).

Now invite along a few outsiders. I like to think of at least two people who could really bring a different perspective to the table. Maybe they work in a creative design team in your company. Maybe they work on another business team but they have a lot of positive energy. If you are ideating in a space that requires expertise, you could even consider bringing in specialists from outside your company. For example, once when I was working on healthy snacks, I brought in a dietician. You could also tap into an agency, supplier, or vendor who has expertise in your category. The only thing to watch out for with true outsiders is they may not understand your strategy and guardrails (and you'll probably need them to sign a legal non-disclosure document).

4. HAVE RULES

If you've invited a broad mix of people to attend your brainstorm, chances are, they will have differing ways of working. It's important to establish how you want your brainstorm to run. Here are the rules I usually establish:

- **A judgment-free zone.** Encourage wild ideas, and don't let anyone start narrowing them down until the end of the brainstorm. If you don't make this a rule, you risk having people make fun of each other's ideas, which can shut down a more sensitive ideator.

- **Listen and build on each other.** When people share their ideas with each other during a brainstorm, I often find someone in the room will have a way to change the idea *slightly* to make it even more exciting ... or more feasible for your company. It's so important to encourage this kind of building. Otherwise, everyone in the room is just waiting their turn to share their *own* brilliant idea and tuning the rest out.

- **No distractions, be fully present.** There is nothing worse than brainstorming with people who are clacking away at their computers or constantly scrolling on their phones. When you invite people to your brainstorm, establish the ground rules for multitasking up front; for example, it's worth suggesting they set their out of office and tell their teams they are tied up for the duration of the brainstorm. If they *must* take a call or answer an email, they *must* leave the room, so it isn't a distraction.

5. SET CLEAR GUARDRAILS

Ummm, we already talked about this once. And we'll revisit it in Chapter Thirteen.

This is a critical part of making your brainstorm effective, so reread Chapter Six or jump to Chapter Thirteen if you want to know more about it now.

6. CREATE AN AGENDA (WITH GREAT IDEATION EXERCISES)

Don't fall into the "go, think, quick" trap. A good brainstorm should be a minimum of three to four hours long, with a variety of exercises planned to help people think about the problem in different ways. Let's look at the key components of a good agenda.

Opener

You'll want to open with a reminder of the strategy and guardrails for the brainstorm, especially if you've invited a broader group to attend. I recommend also having your consumer insights or marketing team present some key insights about the people you are targeting – who they are, what they care about, and what their barriers to purchase and "hates" for your category are. Ask people to take notes during this opener as it will help them later. I'll talk about the importance of consumer insights more in just a second.

Exercises

A good brainstorm will have a series of exercises that are designed to bring out the best creative ideas in your attendees.

By exercises, I mean a framework for how your attendees should come up with creative ideas, so you aren't just asking them to "think about chairs." Below, I've listed examples of effective exercises that I use often, but you can search online and find many more (or hire an innovation agency who are experts in creating these).

===

7 BRAINSTORMING EXERCISES TO BRING OUT THE BEST IN YOUR TEAM

MASH-UPS
» Combine two unrelated products, brands, or ideas to invent something new.
» You can use printed stacks of pictures, actual products out on tables, or lists.
» Example: Given cake mix and an oil spray, I came up with the idea of liquid pancake batter in a spray can.
» This helps you to think outside the box as you'd likely never naturally put these two things together.

REMOVE THE LIMITS
» Have your brainstormers imagine there are no obstacles to their ideas.
» Ask: "If you could do anything, with unlimited time and money, what would you make?"
» You can take this even further than time and money and break the laws of physics or the natural world, heading into science fiction territory.
» This prevents people from putting their own guardrails on their ideas, allowing them to think

more broadly before they need to be whittled down.

REVERSING CATEGORY DISLIKES

» Identify all the key dislikes that your consumers have for your category, using either consumer complaint data your customer service team has or research you've done (see the snack break *Hate, Hate, Hate ... Loathe Entirely*).

» Have teams focus on one dislike at a time and ideate creative ways to improve them.

» This helps to keep your brainstorm focused on your consumers' actual problems, based on data, and will make your ideas more consumer-meaningful.

MATH

» List all the important attributes of innovation in your category (for drinks, this might be that it's portable, cold, bubbly, sweet, or it comes in a can).

» Now have people *subtract* or *multiply* these attributes (whichever you think would work best) to see if the resulting ideas have legs.

» *Subtraction* means you eliminate a key attribute. For example, instead of a fizzy drink being carbonated, it's now flat.

» *Multiplication* means you take an attribute and increase it exponentially. For example, a cold drink becomes a frozen treat or a portable drink that comes in one big can now comes in four smaller ones.

» Math exercises help ideators think outside the box and break category conventions.

BE SPECIFIC

» Create a list of *very* specific ways (occasions) in which your product offering could be used … or people (targets) who could use it (or both).

» Occasion example: while in bathtub soaking sore muscles.

» Target example: firefighters.

» Sometimes, the more outlandish the better.

» Now you have such a specific situation and person to focus on, ask people to come up with an idea that would be perfect for them.

» With outlandish examples especially, this exercise helps unearth ideas that wouldn't have come up otherwise – such as quick-dry clothes you can wear in the bath (allowing you to jump out and escape if the fire alarm goes off).

MEDITATION ON MEMORIES

» This tool is useful if the products in your category can be tied to childhood, family, or specific memorable situations in any way because it's more likely to produce meaningful ideas that resonate with consumers.

» Have a moderator lead the team in meditation on a specific, relevant memory that is tied to the category.

» Ask them to remember all the details around that moment, how they felt, and what was important to them.

» Then ask them to journal about the memory while it's fresh in their minds; afterward, they can use their memories as fodder for ideas.

» If there is time, break the team into small groups and ask them to share their memories to find common themes.

» This helps to humanize the experience of using the product, which helps your attendees empathize with the needs and wants of the consumer.

FORCED QUANTITY

» In a short amount of time (with a timer set), force your ideators to come up with a large number of ideas – perhaps 25 ideas in three minutes.

» This might sound a bit like the "go, think, quick" approach. But it works well as a *single exercise* within a broader brainstorm agenda. The reason is, at idea number 25, people will start to get desperate, and they will push past the obvious to the ideas that are truly creative and unique.

» Ask everyone to sort through their pile and share the best ideas they thought of.

» Look for the diamonds in the rough in this one.

Right, let's get back to the agenda!

Your first exercise of the day should be an individual one.

First thing in the morning (because, remember, your brainstorm should happen in the morning), it is best to start with an exercise allowing everyone to work on their own. This allows each individual to think about your strategy and guardrails and come up with their own solutions based on their unique perspective *before* it becomes contaminated by other people's ideas and groupthink. Often, I find that some of the very best ideas come from this first exercise, so it should not be rushed.

This also allows people to brain dump all the ideas they came up with in advance of your brainstorm. Some of these are the obvious ones (which may be brilliant and just really hard to solve) or they may be breakfast pizza. It's good to empty people's brains of the ideas they walked in with; otherwise, I find they will keep pushing those ideas all day.

Now it's time to put people into teams. Never keep the same people together for the whole brainstorm; keep mixing them up.

Working in teams is hard. As humans, we naturally annoy each other, especially when we spend a lot of time together. And we also tend to think our own ideas are the best ones and other people's ideas aren't as great. If you leave a group of people together for an entire brainstorm, they will drive each other nuts; by the end, they'll be pretty ineffective.

There are also power dynamics in teams, where more extraverted or bossy people take control of the ideation, holding back quieter or more junior folks who may have fantastic ideas. Mixing up the teams means mixing up the dynamics; in this way, you get broader participation.

Energy

Think about energy as you plan your agenda. Tired people are not creative people.

Start with simpler exercises, and make them more creative as the day goes on. This will keep people engaged and help them come up with different ideas.

Food and drink is also a key component of energy. It's also a really effective way of keeping people happy and engaged:

- If you start early, have a high-protein but not-too-heavy breakfast available. You don't want hunger to distract your team.
- Caffeine should be readily available in the room all day, both in the form of coffee and a variety of sodas and energy drinks (people are VERY particular about their caffeine). This will help give people the pep they need to tap into their creativity.
- There should also be water, including the sparkly kind that energizes us non-caffeine drinkers! Water with benefits like electrolytes is a bonus!
- Make sure there is candy on tap; you'd be surprised at what a mood booster this is.
- Lunch should be early – never late. If you have an ideation that goes on until 12:30 pm, no good ideas will come from your hangry crowd.

Take breaks to give your team a chance to rest their brains, but don't let them be energy-sucking-check-your-email-and-realize-what-you-are-missing breaks.

Here are some ideas to make sure breaks invigorate people instead:

- Make them build-your-own-awesome-snack breaks (provide fun mix-ins for topping foods like: oatmeal, popcorn, ice cream, or granola). These can get competitive!
- Arrange to step outside during breaks if that is an option (sunshine is rejuvenating).
- Encourage people to stand rather than sit to get their blood flowing and their energy going again.
- Play a game as a group! I will talk more about this in number 9, the "Have some freakin' fun!" section.

HUMANS NEED LITTLE THINGS, LIKE FOOD AND WATER (AND COFFEE!)

7. INCORPORATE CONSUMER LEARNING

I already mentioned this above as part of the right agenda. In your opener, use consumer research to paint a picture of who your target is and what their consumer needs are.

But what if you don't have that stuff? What if you are a small company and you don't have a consumer insights person or any research to draw on? What if this brainstorm is on a rush timeline and there's no time to pull all that together?

Then plan an inspirational consumer learning activity.

If you are holding a virtual brainstorm, this will have to be work your attendees do on their own before you meet. And you'll tell people up front that the first activity of the day will be for everyone to share what they observed and learned on their individual assignment.

If you are meeting in person, plan a field trip (ideally with a short travel time).

I recommend doing the field trip the day before the brainstorm, so the learning is fresh when you arrive at the ideation session first thing in the morning. If that isn't possible, then do your field trip halfway through your brainstorm, so it can inspire new ideas when the group is running out of steam. You don't want the field trip to be first thing in the morning because, remember, that is the best time to ideate, and you want to get those great ideas out right away!

Individual assignments (for virtual) or field trips (for in person) can be the same types of activities. They can be as simple as going to a few stores and having people either buy or take pictures of products they are inspired by ... *especially* ones that are *not* in your category. And you don't have to go to "normal" stores we are all familiar with. It can be great to go to local specialty stores; they might have more cutting-edge products in your category.

If you sell a service or are an online business, curate a list of competitive websites and have people "shop" them in small groups, so they can get the consumer experience firsthand.

If you are working on improving or creating a benefit with your product, visit a small local business that delivers that same benefit but isn't in your category. For example, if you want to make your product "more convenient," go to a super-fast restaurant, and see how they do it.

This works so well because humans are great at creating parallels. We can find the relevant lessons from an experience

– even if we are looking at unrelated categories – and then think about how to reapply it to our own business.

I find hands-on activities, in particular, really open minds. If you can fit one in your agenda (or schedule it before the brainstorm), do it!

8. PROVIDE A TEMPLATE TO CAPTURE IDEAS

When people imagine a brainstorming session, they think of sticky notes. But when people write down their ideas on these tiny pieces of paper, in fragments of sentences, they do not make sense to anyone the day after (and they'll likely be easily lost).

Instead, I'd highly recommend creating a template of some sort, so your brainstormers can capture their ideas in a more effective way. The simplest template may just have two sections: the name of the idea and a detailed description of the idea. However, you probably want more than that.

Visuals are so powerful. I always recommend asking for a picture, either hand-drawn or pulled from a search engine and attached to the idea. And you may want to list the varieties this idea could come in. It might also help to write down what exercise this idea came from or what part of the strategy. Plus, if you are brainstorming across multiple businesses, what business, brand, and/or category the idea fits under is important for clarity. Think about how you will sort the ideas afterward, and use that to create your ideal template.

Just be warned: Humans are lazy. The more sections you add to an idea template, the less likely they will all get filled in. So, try to keep it to four or five requirements or less.

If you are brainstorming in person, you'll want to print about 150 of these idea templates per day, at least. If you are using an online tool, you can create a template in advance and then have people copy and paste it over and over in the whiteboard.

The next page has an example of a template to capture ideas with five required sections (five pushes the limits of what's feasible). It is available on my website, innovationisugly.com, if you want to download it.

IDEA SHEET
PLEASE PRINT LEGIBLY

I CALL THIS IDEA:

DESCRIBE THIS IDEA IN DETAIL:

BRAINSTORM EXERCISE THIS CAME FROM:

HERE'S A PICTURE OR DRAWING OF THE IDEA:

VARIETIES THIS IDEA COULD COME IN:

9. HAVE SOME FREAKIN' FUN!

Brainstorming sounds fun, doesn't it? But here's another ugly truth. In reality, it's *exhausting*. For both the planners and the attendees. That is, unless the attendees are super-extraverted; then they will feed on everyone else's energy and say it was the best day *ever*, having sucked all the life from the rest of us. I'm sure you're getting sick of me reminding you how hard innovation is by now!

Anywho. Fun matters. If you want to keep everyone's energy up, work some fun activities into your agenda.

I have three go-tos, and I plan them into my agenda from the beginning. One is a fun icebreaking opener, one is a silly competition (bonus if you have silly prizes), and the last is theatre games. You can search the internet for all three of those things and easily find ideas that will work for your group's personality.

Of all the theatre games I've played in brainstorms, I would say Zip-Zap-Zop has been the all-star. Your group stands in a circle and throws an imaginary ball around (real ones are a distraction because people miss). As the "ball" is "thrown," you make direct eye contact with the person you are throwing it at and yell "zip." They must "catch" the ball and then pass it on to a different person, yelling "zap." The key is yelling the *right* word as you pass the ball. The first person yells "zip," the next "zap," and the third "zop," and then the pattern keeps repeating. You want to encourage everyone to throw the imaginary ball *quickly,* which makes getting the right word out surprisingly hard. If someone takes too long or says the wrong word, they step out and the circle gets smaller. Then, when there are only a few folks left who are clearly great at the game, you can add "boing" to the mix to make things tougher. "Boing" is a *rejection* of the pass, yelled with your hands in the air to "block" the imaginary ball. Now the passer must pick a different person and be sure to *repeat* the word they were supposed to have said rather than moving onto the next word in the pattern. Even worse, multiple people can "boing" you in a row, so this might end up sounding like: "Zip! Zap! Boing! Zap! Boing! Zap! Zop!" If my explanation sounds too confusing, look up a video on the internet to see it in action. Zip-Zap-Zop works because it's high energy, competitive, and very funny. Even if you are terrible at it, you will be entertained watching the finalists go at it. People tend to laugh pretty hard.

If your brainstorm is super-rushed or your team is super-lame and refuses to play games, then at a minimum, use some fun tactics to split people into teams. This can be a spontaneous thing that brings energy into the room and encourages people to interact. Arrange yourselves by height! Arrange yourselves by birth month! Then count off one-two-three-four to make four groups down the line. You could even split people using wacky categories like dog-people, cat-people, people-only-people, and exotic-pet-people. The possibilities are endless (but the dog people will always be the best).

Congratulations! We made it through the list. The nine things you need to run an *effective* brainstorm. You have all the tools you need.

BUT WHAT ABOUT THE OBSTACLES YOU NEED TO SIDESTEP TO KEEP YOU ON TRACK? HERE'S WHAT TO AVOID TO PROTECT YOUR BRAINSTORM SESSION:

1. Senior leaders

    Senior leaders *love* to come to brainstorms. But be strong; you simply *can't* allow it. They are a huge distraction to attendees and will encourage groupthink because everyone will be tempted to agree with them. You need to keep the seniority levels pretty flat for an effective brainstorm, so everyone feels safe to speak up and be honest.

    Also, unfortunately, because of both their age and their income level, senior leaders are often out of touch with the real lives of the consumers you are targeting. They will have off-strategy (a nice way to say "dumb") ideas and will want to push them.

    If they insist, a good way to appease them is to agree to share the top ideas with them after the brainstorm, either at the end of the last day or shortly thereafter. Another option is to tell them to send you their ideas and then quietly include them in the list you vote on during the brainstorm; alternatively, you could suggest them as though they are your own, so they get in the mix. That way their ideas aren't lost, but also aren't forced to the top of the pile.

2. **Power dot voting**

One approach that is super-common in in-person brainstorms is to hang all the ideas on the wall and then hand out either a sheet of stickers or a bunch of markers and have people "power dot" the best ones – which is a fancy way of saying vote for the ones they like the best (by putting dots or stickers on them).

The problem with voting like this is GROUPTHINK (*said with echoing microphone for dramatic effect*). Groupthink happens because of two natural human behaviors: 1. We want to fit in with the group and feel insecure when we don't, and 2. we are inherently lazy and try to find mental shortcuts when things are hard.

The first leads people to assume the group is probably right and vote accordingly, despite what we may secretly believe. We often doubt ourselves, assuming everyone else is more creative than we are (which isn't very creative as far as insecurities go, ironically). Also, I find many people are afraid to vote for an idea they think no one else likes.

The second behavior (laziness) will cause an overwhelmed person, looking at hundreds of ideas on a wall, to naturally gravitate toward choosing the ones other people have already voted for. It's an obvious mental shortcut.

Instead of power dotting, create some sort of ballot, so people can vote privately and without undue influence. This can literally be a blank piece of paper that each person writes their top five ideas on and hands in. Or, if you have time, type a list of all the ideas that people have had, hand out sheets with them on it, and ask everyone to circle their favorites. Then tally them up. This involves more effort, but I *promise* you that you'll end up with a far broader set of winning ideas this way. I also find that people are more thoughtful in this process, considering every idea equally.

When running a virtual brainstorm, whiteboard tools often have systems for power dotting ideas too. The great news here is they are often anonymous until all votes are revealed, which avoids the problems inherent in in-person power dotting and saves you time tallying votes by hand.

One final thought about voting: Have a rule about how many of their own ideas an attendee can vote for. I usually don't allow them to use more than half their votes on these. Sometimes, faced with a really stubborn or lazy group of people, I will say they can't vote for *any* of their own ideas. Otherwise, some will not even bother to consider other solutions, and it'll be harder for the best ones to float to the top.

3. **Illustrators**

This one will be controversial because it's such a standard way of working for many innovation agencies. But I've never found illustrators add value in a live brainstorm.

Illustrators are inherently creative, meaning they add their own imagination to the mix. They therefore tend to bring ideas to life differently than the ideator intended because they can't help but include their own creative twist. Or it may be that they just don't understand it because it's not theirs.

But what should you do instead?

If you want illustrations of ideas in your brainstorm, the first option is just to accept the amateur, stick-figure-style drawings your attendees will create. Even at their most basic, they usually make the ideas clearer because the individual drawing them understands the idea best.

Do you want more photo-realistic images? If so, allow people to use an online search engine to find relevant visuals. If you are brainstorming in person and don't want people distracted by their own computers (they will likely be tempted to reply to just *one* little email), provide a shared computer in a corner of the room with the search engine page ready and waiting and a printer connected. Most companies have loaners the admins or office managers have access to, and the bonus is they won't have anyone's email loaded onto them. Voila! Perfect pictures for your attendees to attach to their idea templates.

If your brainstorm is virtual, this will be even easier. Most whiteboard tools have the ability to cut and paste images straight from a search engine into the platform. Technology for the win here; now you have easy-to-understand ideas with great images in your idea templates.

PHEW!

Did you get all of that? Nine things **to do** and three things **not to do**. That was a lot.

Brainstorms are *so* important because creativity is hard. It's worth investing in careful planning and genuine inspiration to give your team their best chance to come up with something brilliant.

Well, this chair sucks (no pizza at all) and my butt hurts, so I'm going to take a real-life snack break now. Why don't you join me?

CHAPTER NINE

INNOVATION ISLAND

Here's a question that plagues a lot of executives: How should innovation teams be structured? By this I mean, where do they go in our organization in relation to the resources that support the core part of the business?

One of the most hotly debated structures is the innovation ivory tower. Am I dating myself with that wording? It's the idea of separating innovation teams – be they marketers, R&D developers, engineers, or all of the above – off on an island, alone. However, I like the word "island" better than "tower" because it calls out that these resources are separated from everyone else, so they can prioritize disruptive innovation without being distracted (or, frankly, stopped) from working on such "out there" stuff.

These islands are usually created by executives who feel like there isn't enough "true" innovation coming from the business team. The answer to why big bet innovation isn't happening is almost always the same – the business team has too many other distractions.

Their argument is: *How will we ever produce real breakthroughs and new technologies if we don't dedicate some scientists or engineers to working only on that goal? So, let's carve a team off and send them to a protected island to work alone, right?*

Is this a good idea? Well, it depends, but the answer is usually no. In fact, it's often a very bad idea (even if the innovators look really happy).

Innovation islands *can* work if certain things are true (and these are some very big ifs).

IF this structure has support not just from a mid-level leader but the executive leadership team and board of directors.

Why does this matter? Because on innovation island, the ideas are BIG. Big ideas are damn expensive. They usually require capital and advertising to explain them and a lot of people to make them happen. Without senior buy-in behind innovation island, you won't get any successful launches, just a lot of expensive creativity.

IF the team sent to the island has *clear* guardrails, aligned with the corporate strategy, and isn't just working on whatever "creative" things appeal to them, like turning everything into pizza (see Chapter Six).

IF regular reviews are scheduled with the executive team sponsoring the island, to assess ideas, check on project progress, and reinforce alignment to the overall strategy.

Even if all these things are true, I don't find this situation lasts long at most companies. Having a terrible year? Looking for places to cut cost and headcount? The island team will end up on the chopping block. After all, *nothing* they are working on even affects *this year's plan!*

Or maybe you have a strong business leader who thinks what the innovation island is working on is not at all aligned to their strategy and vision. High tide's coming in.

A lot of the companies I have worked for create and destroy these dedicated "big idea" teams over and over again. If you feel you need one at your company, my recommendation is to set it up as a temporary working team with a one- to two-year scope rather than as a permanent structure. Limit the scope to getting to a reasonable business case, then pull the projects back into the business team. That sets the expectation from the beginning around how often this team will be checked in on and prevents them from running amok.

So, if innovation island is a no-go, what is the ideal innovation structure?

As I've hinted at above, innovation structures often swing like a pendulum in companies. The ideas aren't big or ambitious enough – so they separate innovation out. The ideas aren't strategic enough and lots of time and money are being wasted on things that aren't realistic – so innovation is pulled back into the heart of the business.

The reality is that this pendulum swing happens because *both* extremes are wrong:

- ✓ An innovation team that's fully integrated into the everyday business will *never* prioritize big ideas and long-term innovation enough. There are simply too many short-term priorities. If long-term innovation is only a fraction of some people's time, what are they going to focus on? The issues that are breathing down their necks ... and the fixes that need to be in market this year.

- ✓ An innovation team on an island will drift from the mainland. Communication lines will get weaker over time and a sense of "us" vs. "them" will hurt collaboration.

So, what do you do? **The ideal, in my opinion, is a matrixed innovation structure.**

These still have dedicated innovators, ideally in teams, but those teams report into their respective business directly. That reporting structure ensures seamless communication with the business, alignment on strategy and objectives, and enough independence to be able to focus on truly big ideas without distractions. If you're truly committed to building an innovation engine firing on all cylinders, this gives you the best of both worlds.

I've worked in all three of these structures.
- To be honest, the island was by far the most *fun*. Blast, there's that word again (but seriously, in one of them we had a team shot ski).
- The integrated structure was the most challenging; everything big I worked on kept getting delayed due to prioritization.
- In the matrixed roles, I accomplished the most. Period.

MATRIXED
INNOVATION TEAMS

BUSINESS TEAMS

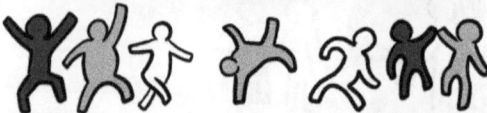

OUR
INNOVATION
IS STRATEGIC!

DEDICATED INNOVATION
TEAMS REPORTING TO BUSINESS

If you need to produce truly disruptive projects, and your innovation team is running flat out, you could consider a matrixed team *plus* a small island that is dedicated to riskier and big bet innovation. But you must still give the small island a clear, time-bound scope.

If you are truly dedicated to growth through innovation, *prove it –* *not* by building an island fortress but by setting up a smart matrix, designed to win.

CHAPTER TEN

INNOVATION IS ALREADY AGILE: KEEP STEALING IDEAS FROM DESIGN THINKING

For a long time, I was sick and tired of people saying the following buzzwords to me: sprint, agile, and design thinking. When executives asked me about these, it felt like they were really just saying, "You can go faster!"

However, in 2019, I had the distinct honor of running an agile innovation lab. It was a cross-functional team of designers, chefs, marketers, R&D developers, project managers, and consumer insights professionals. We leveraged the principles of design thinking and "big A" Agile, ran sprints (I'll explain what all of this means in a second), and generally had an amazing time doing it. The innovation lab was one of the most fun innovation islands I've ever had the pleasure to live on.

In that job, I learned a lot more about the true meaning of these buzzwords and have come to believe a few things:

1. Product innovation typically **already leverages design thinking principles**.
2. There are some **classic sprint tools that innovators can leverage** to make their brainstorms (and project strategies) even more effective.

Let's break these two down. First, we are *already agile*. We don't need to overhaul our approach the way software engineers did in the early 2000s. We don't need it explained to us that the consumer should be at the center of our innovation work. We *already know* project managers are the secret weapon to success. The only difference we have with Silicon Valley is that most of us can't do a two-week sprint on a project because software prototyping just requires people time whereas product prototyping typically requires more resources.

However, there are some very specific Agile approaches to brainstorming and project strategies that can work very well for us ... *especially* if we are working on truly disruptive innovation.

Before we dive into these tools, let's take a step back and better understand the concepts.

What is Agile?

The term "Agile" comes from a manifesto 17 software developers wrote in 2001. They were unhappy with how software innovation was happening and wanted to rethink the approach to ensure it was truly functional. For example, they felt it should be developed in collaboration with users and more responsive to market changes. Frankly, they proposed things that seem obvious to us as product innovators. That's why I feel quite comfortable saying that product innovation is *already agile*.

But the concept of Agile is often tied to the idea of going *faster*. That is because one of its other principles is *iteration*. In order to create effective software that considers the end user and is responsive to market changes, you need to create a prototype and test it. Then you'll use that consumer learning to prototype again and test again. You rinse and repeat these steps (quickly) until you have something that works.

Agile also calls for a collaborative, cross-functional team that is dedicated to the project and organized by a project manager. This team will be all-hands-on-deck for the entire (fast-paced) project, with no handoffs. The team is also often fully dedicated to one project, very flat in structure (everyone has the same boss vs. having different bosses for each function), and self-organized rather than hierarchical. This is similar to product innovation in some ways, but in true Agile teams, members don't stay in their lanes. Everyone helps with everything. That doesn't happen in most product manufacturing corporations.

So, how do sprints and design thinking fit into all this?

Agile tends to go hand in hand with the concept of design thinking. Design thinking is exactly what it sounds like – using the way designers, artists, and creators are trained to think in art schools and infusing it into how we think about innovation. It's all about staying human-centric and focusing on the human need.

Check (we already do that).

So, how is design thinking *different* from what we do every day in product innovation? Classic design thinking follows a unique process and a sprint methodology.

There are different definitions of the design thinking process and what a "design sprint" is. Typically, however, it involves something like these five steps below.

1. **Consumer research**
2. **Research analysis and synthesis**
    a. Create a persona
    b. Map the consumer journey
    c. Write "how might we" problem statements
3. **Problem (re)definition**
4. **Prototyping**
5. **Testing**

As I've mentioned, those last two steps will repeat until you identify a solution to the problem. Does this sound very similar to what you already do in product innovation? Probably. I would argue the macro difference comes in steps 2 and 3. In product innovation, we usually do some research, assume we know what the problem is we are solving, and then jump right into prototyping.

So, what can product innovators learn from this approach?

That leads me to the tools that could help us product innovators working on truly disruptive innovation, projects that would benefit from us pushing the boundaries of typical thinking.

Let's start by looking at **Step 1, consumer research.** Design thinking teaches us that consumer research should build deep empathy with our subjects. That means it shouldn't just be a survey with a large base size or online focus groups. It also means you aren't just asking about your own category and what they think of it or how they use it.

Instead, you spend more time with consumers, learning their stories and really getting to know them. You could do this by using a methodology like ethnography, where researchers spend time interviewing individuals or groups in their home environments to learn about the motivation behind their habits and practices. Design thinking also has a point of view on who the *right* consumers are to talk to. In my snack break after Chapter Seven, *Hate, Hate, Hate … Loathe Entirely*, I talked about hate research using extreme consumers – this idea comes from this approach. In design thinking, you would never focus on *average* consumers the way we often do in product innovation research. You want to talk to the lovers, the haters, the experts, the leaders, the rejectors, and the laggards. Why? Because they will have the most interesting stories. They have true emotion for your category (even if that emotion is *hate!*).

When you talk to folks on the extremes, you will gather tons of insights.

This is when it's time for Step 2, research analysis and synthesis.

In a design sprint, you would then take time to really break down these insights and examine them. Do this as a team (not just you and your best friend in insights) because everyone needs to have the same foundational consumer empathy. Not everyone will have attended or read through all the research, so it's also helpful to review what you learned from the extreme users you talked to (both lovers and haters, hopefully) together.

Then you should work together to create a **persona**. This is similar to a consumer target, but it is much more complex and nuanced than throwing together some demographics. It should get to the consumer's "big <u>why</u>" … their true <u>need</u> for your category. This answers why they do what they do, and it's usually for a deep emotional reason, i.e., fear, love, or belonging. Hopefully, by talking to extreme consumers who express passion, you will be able to see these big whys come to life.

Now *name* your persona. The name should summarize their big why, and it should be really clear to the whole team. For example, something like: "security-conscious fragile seniors." In a typical product innovation, we might say we are targeting "65+ independents." See how much more emotion is in the persona name?

Next, outline the **consumer journey** that a person takes to get to your category. This does *not* mean a map between their house and the store, the way marketing agencies think about journeys. Instead, this can often be described as a "life map" that tracks the ups and downs of their life, zoomed in on the stage they are in. For example, multiple times in my career, I've been reminded that there is a trigger that occurs when most people reach their 40s that encourages them to start paying more attention to what they are eating. That trigger might be that their pants don't fit anymore, that their parents are in poor health, or that they receive some bad blood work results (like high cholesterol). Whatever it is, it happens frequently at this milestone in our lives, and importantly, it is often very emotional. Consumers don't typically change their behavior based on logic alone. This health trigger drives 40-somethings to suddenly eat kale, for goodness' sake, when we all know it's something that should remain as a non-edible garnish on a buffet plate!

Once you identify these big or small changes that consumers go through and outline the consumer journey for your persona, go back through all of your research with a fine-tooth comb. Capture all the insights, group them, and give those insight bundles titles. You can then turn those insights into **problem statements** phrased as questions, using the **"how might we"** structure.

This is a departure from the typical product innovation approach, where you would go from insights straight to ideas. In design thinking, you stop to really think about the <u>problem</u>.

For example, if you have a bundle of insights around how young, first-time parents try to carry their whole life around with them everywhere they go (in their pockets or car or bags or purse), you might write: "How might we help parents carry less?" Or if you've learned that there's a special bond dads create with their kids by buying them pizza, you might write: "How might we create a 'pizza bond' between dads and their kids through something other than food?" This "how might we" approach tends to be *far* more specific and inspiring than the problem statements we write as product innovators based on talking to average consumers. As an example, we might write: "What's the next evolution of diapers?" This feels more like a "go, think, quick" problem statement. "How might we" questions drive inspiration because they take you right to the heart of the consumer's unmet need: "How might we design a diaper that comforts a sick baby?"

As a side note, if you do nothing more than add a step to your current front-end innovation process where you create "how might we" questions as part of your standard brainstorms, you will still get a *lot* out of this. I think it's a great jumping-off point for ideation.

Now you are ready to complete Step 3, problem (re)definition.

Narrow your "how might we" questions down to the most powerful. There might be one that towers above the rest, but you may have several that feel like really good territory for ideation. Use them to frame **the key problem you want to solve in your category**.

Remember, solving consumer frustrations or unmet needs is the *best* way to deliver truly incremental innovation. Write up this problem and tuck the associated "how might we" questions underneath it. It might look something like this (I haven't done in-depth research about TVs with consumers, so forgive me if it's a bad example, but I wanted something we could hopefully all relate to):

Problem: Consumers HATE television remotes

- ✓ How might we speed up time from consumer desire to TV reaction?
- ✓ How might we keep remotes from ever getting lost?
- ✓ How might we make TV remote buttons less confusing?
- ✓ How might we eliminate remotes completely?

Now you can relax and return to your regularly scheduled innovation program.

Those are the tools from Agile and design thinking approaches that I find most helpful for product innovation. The prototype, test, repeat steps aren't always appropriate for us, but if they make sense for your project, follow the whole design sprint process!

So, in summary, here are the key approaches to making your product innovation *even more agile*:

- Consider talking to extreme users rather than average ones.
- Use research tools that help you learn those people's "stories" and build empathy for them.
- Do an in-depth, full-team debrief of your research, looking for insight nuggets.
- Build out a consumer persona, including their <u>big why</u> for using your category and their journey in life to get to their need(s).
- Write out "how might we" questions to address your learning from the insights.
- Think about consumer problems deeply before jumping to ideas.

If you are pursuing this type of work for the first time, I highly recommend hiring a design thinking expert to help guide your team. There are tons of innovation agencies out there that can lead you through a design sprint. My only caution is that this depth of work is best for disruptive innovation – your big bets. Using it for simple line extensions is overkill.

On the other hand, if you are asked to "be agile" – *not* in order to be more creative, but just to go *faster* – then consider focusing on these aspects of the agile process instead:

- Fully dedicate a cross-functional team to your project, so they can focus only on this goal.
- Structure it as a flat team with one leader, even though they all come from different functions (it will make decision-making much faster).
- Give them a strong project manager to lead them through the process, so they can't get off track.
- Find ways to prototype as fast as possible (maybe through outside vendors and contract manufacturers), so you can iterate using consumer testing.

I hope that helped demystify Agile, sprints, and design thinking.

My goal is that you'll better understand these buzzwords and what executives are driving at when they throw them your way. Now you can push back on the request to leverage them, explaining that your innovation process is *already* agile, or you can cherry-pick the best tools from this stable to turbocharge your more disruptive projects.

— SNACK BREAK —

EMBRACE THE TEAM VENN

My best friend and I like to use Venn diagrams to describe our friendship (my best friend and I are nerds).

Venn diagrams use overlapping circles to represent the relationship between two different things. The area in the middle, where they overlap, describes what they have in common, and the two parts that don't overlap, at each side, describe what is different.

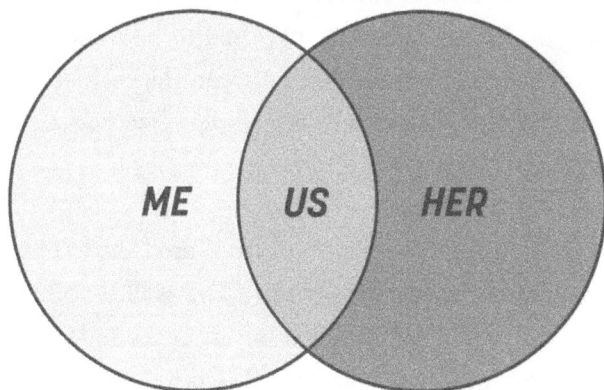

ME   US   HER

In my Venn diagram with my best friend, the overlapping sections includes things like pizza, cocktails, people watching, working too much, and loving our hilarious children. But, to be honest, there's a lot more we don't agree on. She hates a lot of the things I love, including theatre, shellfish, reading, and the color red. Similarly, I wouldn't be caught dead in half the outfits she wears (camo at our age?!), and she likes string cheese in a way I consider unnatural (I can say that because we also disagree on reading. She will never get this far into this book).

Why am I rambling about my weird friendship?

Because I'm tired of innovation teams being split down the middle based on their differences. There's the technical team (R&D, engineering, manufacturing, quality, supply – aka the builders) and the commercial team (marketing, sales, insights, finance – aka the sellers). If I didn't include your function, my sincere apologies, but you can probably place yourself on one side or the other. In my oversimplified Venn, the builders figure out *how* we can bring an idea to life, and the sellers convince everyone it's the right thing to do, both in and outside of the company.

As you read this, whatever side you are on, ask yourself this: At your company, do you feel like you are supposed to hate the people on the other side? Is there a lot of conflict between the teams? Do you have conflicting priorities? Does it sometimes feel like you are speaking a different language?

Although I wish it wasn't so, I bet you answered yes to at least one of those. Unfortunately, this divide is alive and well. It often shows up when innovation projects hit a speed bump, and one team blames the other to avoid taking accountability. This never ends well. There's a quote by Jim Rohn that I love: **"Excuses are the nails used to build the** house of failure." The type of culture bred by the "blame game," with low levels of trust and collaboration, is the *worst* culture to nurture big innovation. You'll be lucky to even get big ideas out the door, and you'll be even luckier if they work.

Here's something I've learned over and over throughout a long career in innovation.

When those involved in innovation act like they are *one team*, united behind common goals, they will be an *unstoppable force*.

And the truth is, you have So. Much. In. Common. I bet you all like pizza, don't you? (It's creative food, remember?) Focus on the things you agree on.

You are all curious and want to chase big, creative ideas. Yes, you are creative in different ways, but that's why you are a good team. You balance each other out.

You are all analytical, evaluating the market opportunities and finding the gaps. Yes, you have different metrics you focus on when you evaluate the market, but that's why you are a good team. You balance each other out.

You all want your innovation to be successful and are passionate and courageous in your convictions. But you can't do it alone. You need each other. Be a good teammate. If you do the opposite and lean into the differences between you, embracing conflict and the blame game, you will fail *far* more often.

So, if you are unfortunate enough to work in a company with a long history of conflict between the technical and commercial teams, what do you do?

It can take quite a bit of trust-building and maybe some swallowed pride to build an initial connection, but it's worth it. Become best-friends-at-work with your peers on the other side of the Venn. You'll find you can make big, complicated, hard (and, dare I say it, *fun*) innovation happen together. You'll suddenly be able to see all sides of the problem (because of how you think differently) and you'll find creative solutions (because of your shared convictions and goals).

Embrace the Venn. Be unstoppable.

THE INNOVATOR VENN DIAGRAM

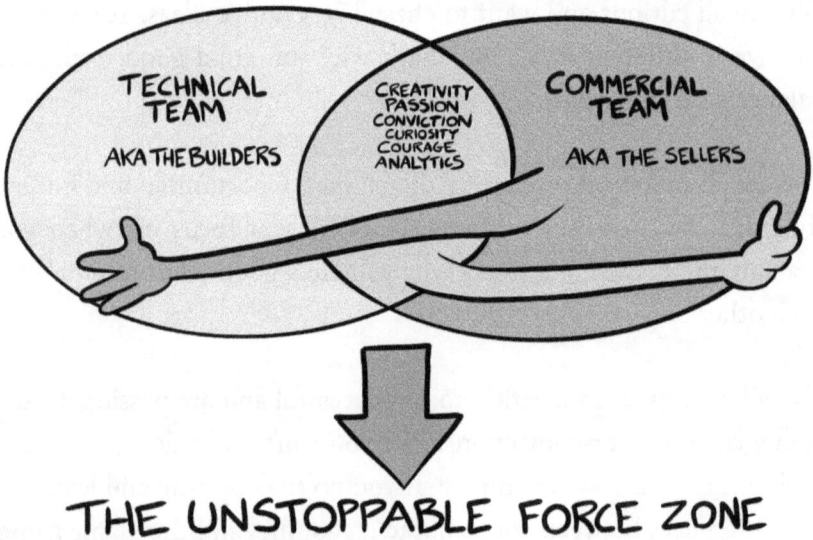

TECHNICAL TEAM

AKA THE BUILDERS

CREATIVITY
PASSION
CONVICTION
CURIOSITY
COURAGE
ANALYTICS

COMMERCIAL TEAM

AKA THE SELLERS

THE UNSTOPPABLE FORCE ZONE

CHAPTER ELEVEN

SAY LESS! WRITING SIMPLE, STRONG INNOVATION CONCEPTS

Confidence is key. Both in life and innovation. Confident people make friends more easily. Confident people convince peers of their point of view more often. Confident people just seem to be more successful, don't they?

But one very specific thing I've noticed is that confident people tend to *say less*. They don't over-explain, driven by insecurity or nervousness. They just state their truths, concisely. And if we're all honest, that's attractive. It draws you in. It makes you listen when they do speak. We could learn a lot from confident people when we write our innovation concepts because they are all about convincing consumers to like you. To want you.

Honestly, this *could* be a really short chapter. I could just tell you to "say less" when writing innovation concepts, and that would be the end of it. That's the gist. Short concepts score best. I know this because I once had a curious insights lead who partnered with me to definitively prove this. We tested the same ideas with more adjective-laden, verbose descriptions against very simple, straightforward ones.

Consumers preferred the simple ideas. Every time. It wasn't even close.

This is another "how to" chapter that less experienced innovators will probably find most helpful. So let's back up a second. **Do you know what an innovation concept is?**

It's an "about me" or a "profile" for an innovation idea that you use to explain it to consumers to get their reactions. It's typically a single picture with a description next to it or just a few sentences that describe the innovation with no picture. After they review it, consumers then rank it/score it/tell-you-if-it-sucks. In product innovation, we often test batches of concepts in order to fill our pipeline in an organized way. Typically, you would do this once a year, after an excellent brainstorm (or two). If you *aren't* testing your ideas with consumers or foodservice operators or experts or your neighbors … why not? It might help you pick stronger ideas to work on.

Anyway, let's get back to it: Why should those concepts be short? Sure, confidence is key, and confident people say less, but let's dive a little deeper than that.

1. Our attention spans are short

And they're only getting shorter in the social media age. We are all shopping online while watching TV and messaging our friends these days. You might be doing all of that while reading this book! Our brains are overwhelmed, and our thoughts are divided and unfocused.

Once it's out in the real world, your product will be seen by a consumer in passing, either online or on a shelf or in an ad. Probably for only a few seconds. And they will only really engage and remember that innovation if it instantly grabs their attention. If it doesn't tell you what it is quickly and clearly, it doesn't have a chance. The problem is, if your concept over-explains what your idea is (maybe because it's a complicated idea), it may test well in research, but when you only have three seconds to explain it in the real world, consumers may not get it at all.

2. The average reading level in the U.S. is equivalent to that of a middle-school student

You might be shocked to hear this, but those statistics haven't moved much as I've checked them over the years. That means if you write a diatribe filled with exquisite, egregious, efficacious, gustatory, loquacious, mendacious, or sagacious adjectives that most people don't understand, your idea will fail.

So, the rule is: Keep it simple. But do you know what's simpler than reading? Looking at a picture. And that's why I recommend focusing on visuals rather than text in your innovation concept. It's true what they say: A picture is worth a thousand words. And it's a hell of a lot less boring than reading for most people.

So, how do we put together an innovation concept based on these core truths?

Here are my **five recommended approaches** that will engage your audience and convey the product idea clearly (in priority order):

1. **Pack shot and price.** For product innovation, this would be a picture of the package as it would appear on the shelf, with the price below it. There should be no other information. This is the best approach, as it simulates how consumers will be exposed to your idea in real life.

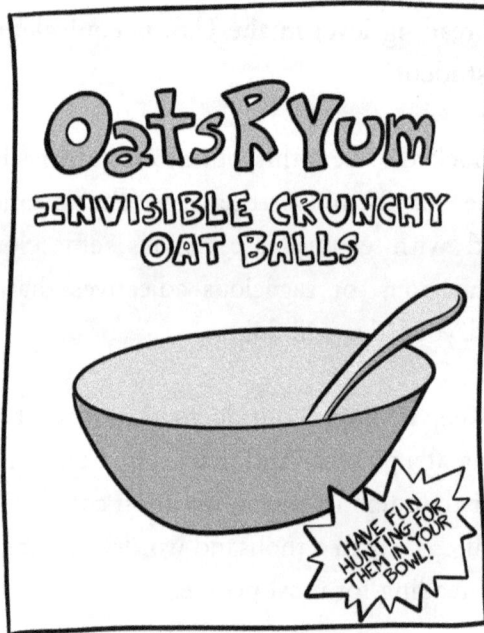

PRICE: $6.99

2. **Pack shot and finished product picture and price.** This is the same as 1 but with a larger picture of the finished product. In most cases, the finished product is what appears on the package, so this approach shouldn't be necessary ... but if your category is an exception, this can be a helpful option. For example, a lot of candy wrappers are too small to show a picture of the product on them. So, if you were testing a new candy, you might show the package plus a shot of the unwrapped candy.

3. **A picture and one-sentence description and price.** Don't sell with your description. Just explain, in simple words, exactly what the idea is.

4. **A one- to three-sentence description and price.** This no-picture option is near the bottom of the list because visuals are the most powerful tool to convey ideas. Few innovations are sold without a visual because they are new to the consumer and need explanation, so using an image is a no-brainer (unless you are selling a service). Innovators often choose this option because they are too lazy to hire a proper illustrator. Without a visual, you'll probably need two sentences to effectively explain the idea.

KIDS LOVE MAGIC.

NEW, FROM OatsRYum, A CEREAL WITH MAGICAL PROPERTIES—IT'S INVISIBLE!

THESE CRUNCHY OAT BALLS ARE DELICIOUS, AND YOUR KIDS WILL HAVE FUN HUNTING FOR THEM IN THEIR BOWL.

---

5. **A prototype.** This option requires either in-person testing (with physical prototypes) or a virtual 3-D model that consumers can react to online. This is best suited to truly disruptive and/or complex innovation that is too hard to understand without interacting with it. However, it will be expensive and time-consuming, so it's overblown for anything that fits neatly into an existing category.

One thing I haven't added to this list is video concepts. Unless you are spending a boatload on advertising to introduce this idea to the world, this option will overstate consumer interest in and understanding of your idea (because your actual consumers won't be getting this five-star treatment). And that is a good reminder to think about how your product will be sold in market. If your innovation will not have advertising, you should always pick option 1. You want this test to be realistic in terms of what will actually happen when it hits the shelves.

So, we've talked about a lot of **critical components of innovation concepts**, including pictures, prices, names, and descriptions. Let's dive into each of these and how to maximize their impact.

1. Pictures
2. Price
3. Name of the innovation as concept headline
4. Description
   a. Opening insight
   b. Benefit
   c. Reason(s) to believe (RTBs)
5. Variants
6. All other key details

1. PICTURES

- Pictures are critical. They should be photos or photo-realistic sketches in order to convey the concept clearly and engage people. In my long career, I've watched over and over while innovators hired sub-par illustrators to make confusing or ugly sketches; and then they wonder why their great ideas didn't test well. Finding an illustrator that can make photo-realistic images can be hard. It might also be expensive. But it's 100%

worth it. If you can't find someone, it's better to pull images off a search engine than to test bad sketches.

- They should show the product on/in its packaging, so it's a realistic portrayal of how the consumer will interact with it.

- The picture should take up as much of the total concept image as possible.

- Package shots are much better than a picture of the product with no context as they can be misleading (for example, if I show you a picture of a cake, you may think I'm selling you a pre-made bakery item rather than a cake mix).

- Package shots should include the claim you put on the front panel that explains the benefit of the new item (the way it will be explained in market).

2. PRICE

- Including a price is important because if you are way outside the range of what someone will pay for the item, it's important to know that early. If you don't include a price, your purchase interest scores aren't valid. For example, imagine a new soft drink you test does extremely well with consumers but you don't mention that it costs an eye-watering $10 a can.

- However, price points should be on the low end of realistic. You don't want your concept to fail just because of price in the first round of testing. You can optimize pricing based on market comparisons later.

- If you are testing a product with kids, you should not include a price (they aren't paying, so price doesn't influence their decision).

3. NAME OF THE INNOVATION AS CONCEPT HEADLINE

- Testing sometimes utilizes headlines that sum up what a product does, but I don't subscribe to this approach anymore because that's not how real life works (there's no large headline floating above a shelf in the store). The product's name is the first thing consumers will see, so *the name is your headline.*

- It helps to have the product name at the top of your concept in this way because you will keep referring to the idea by that name in testing, and this will avoid confusion.

- The name should be what would appear on the package, without a bunch of adjectives added in front of it. Again, this is about reflecting how that product will be experienced in real life.

4A. DESCRIPTION – OPENING INSIGHT

- An opening insight summarizes the key consumer learning that led to this idea.

- As I've said, *less is more, so keep this short.*

- Alternatively, don't include it at all. I don't buy into the outdated thinking that you *must* open your concept with a consumer insight or problem. If you make the mistake of opening with a misjudged insight, this could upend the whole process because it will immediately make your consumers defensive. Here are two examples of bad opening insights I've seen in the past:
  - "Do you get sick of your kids sometimes and just need a dad-break?" *Um, no, I'm an excellent parent. How dare you!*
  - "Are you tired of the same old pasta options?" *Not even a little bit; I could eat pesto fettucine all day, every day. This product obviously isn't for me.*

- So, if you do open with an insight, approach it carefully, following these tips:
  - ○ The insight opening should set up either an issue or an opportunity for your brand. This must be a compelling and universal truth or problem that won't divide people. For example, "Women try to fit too much into their purses," or, "There simply aren't enough hours in the day," or, "Kids love magic." Most parents won't fight with you on that one.
  - ○ Express it as a question to engage the consumer: "Do you try to fit too much into your purse?" And then provide an answer that describes the benefit of your product: "Introducing PurseSquares, the most organized purse ever made."

4B. DESCRIPTION – BENEFIT

- Now you want to describe the solution this innovation is providing to the consumer. This is essential if you don't have an image. If you do have an image, remember, *less is more, so keep this short.*

- As you'll remember from Chapter Seven, the point of difference for your product should be consumer-driven and meaningful, ownable, and single-minded. So, this should not be a list of *all* the benefits of the product. Single-minded means *one* benefit. If it wouldn't be mentioned on the front panel (prominently) or in advertising, it shouldn't go in the concept either.

- A benefit should describe what something *does* for the consumer, not what something *is*. It's not just a description of the product. So, for our cereal, the benefit isn't that it's invisible, it's *why* being invisible *matters*. The benefit is that hunting for cereal with your spoon is fun. It's about play.

- The benefit can be either functional ("cleans better") or

emotional ("peace of mind"), depending on your category and your product.

- Note that if you are writing a concept to test with a third party and not the end user – a mom for their kid, a doctor for their patient, a distributor for their stores, or a foodservice operator for their customer – you will need to list the benefit to *both* them *and* the end user (in this case, make sure you know what that third party cares about as well as the end user – usually things like cost, accuracy, ease of use, and employee time).

4C. DESCRIPTION – REASON(S) TO BELIEVE (RTBS)

- Reasons to believe are the product attributes that build the credibility of your benefit (they can be as much of a mouthful as this sentence if you aren't careful).

- Have I mentioned *less is more*? Ha. But seriously, keep this part short too, or don't include it at all.

- Critically, reasons to believe should only be in the concept if they would be in the advertising. For example, I didn't explain the technology behind our invisible cereal because we wouldn't do that on the pack or in advertising (if you are wondering what it is, that's proprietary. I can't tell you, or I'd have to disappear *you*).

- Typically, important RTBs are things like:
  o **Ingredients** that either are or *are not* in the product. Things like "allergen free," "made with Pro-V® vitamins," "zero calories," or "contains *no* bleach."
  o **Heritage.** For example, it's still made with the original, 50-year-old formula. Or how long you've been in business serving this market.
  o **Claims.** Better, faster, cleaner, stronger, smarter.

- If your category comes with a lot of consumer skepticism or concern, RTBs might be really important. For example, an auto-shut off promise on a space heater may reassure those worried about fire safety.

- If your benefit isn't ownable, your RTB might be the ownable part of your idea. When that is the case, you should definitely highlight the RTB to explain why the product is able to deliver on this benefit. For example, the cereal is fun (a benefit that isn't ownable) because it's magically invisible (a super-unique and ownable RTB).

5. VARIANTS

- If your innovation is launching as part of a full line, with several varieties, it may be important to list what those varieties are (because your picture should only show one).

- But this is a slippery slope! The more varieties you list, the better your concept will test (there's something for everyone!), which may skew your scores. So, only list as many as you will *actually* launch, not as many as you are currently considering or exploring. It must reflect reality in order to provide accurate results.

- For the same reason, if there is one variant that is likely to always be the hero in advertising and in market, just show that one for the concept test.

6. ALL OTHER KEY DETAILS

- Honestly, if you can include nothing else, that's great! *Less is more.*

- However, sometimes it's important to explain *how* to use or prepare your innovation, *where* you would use it, or *when* you would use it.

- Only include these additional details if the consumer won't understand your idea without them (and, of course, if they would make it on the front of the package or into advertising).

- Some examples of critical additional details could include a product that requires a certain piece of equipment (slow cooker, air fryer), one that requires assembly, one that is safe under water, or one that works with most smart home systems. These are facts unrelated to the benefits (so are not RTBs), but they might be critical for the consumer to understand the idea and rate its appeal to them.

We're almost there, but I have *one final note* on writing innovation concepts.

Concepts are different from ads. Advertising can be silly, goofy, eye-rolly, and overzealous … and we can forgive it. After all, it's trying to entertain us – so we don't take it too seriously.

When we write concepts, it is not for entertainment; it is for the sole purpose of consumer testing. You are going to ask a consumer to sit down and read this concept carefully, with a critical eye, so you can ask a whole bunch of questions about what they thought of it. If it comes across as inauthentic, trying too hard, silly, or annoying, consumers will pan it.

Here's a story that illustrates that divergence perfectly. I worked on a brand that had a successful and very funny advertising campaign. It scored highly in advertising testing, and it drove growth on the brand. I started including the funny tagline they used in their advertising in my innovation concepts. They scored *worse* than they did without it. In fact, the tagline was listed as one of the most disliked parts of the concept! It may seem crazy, but it's a testament to how people approach innovation testing. When they are participating in research, consumers know they're being asked to be judgmental, and they are *serious* about that task! So, don't mess around with inserting advertising copy – just stick to the facts about the idea.

That's it. Go write your *short, simple* concepts with **confidence.** I hope consumers love them!

— SNACK BREAK —

WHAT TO DO WITH "FREE IDEAS" FROM EXECUTIVES

When you work in innovation, everywhere you go, people will suggest ideas to you. Your friends. Your family. Your neighbors. And your leadership team.

Now, I firmly believe **ideas come from everywhere**. As a leader in innovation, you should be open to ideas from your key partners across all functions; in fact, you should be actively involving them in brainstorms. You should also listen to the technical experts at your manufacturing facilities talk about what *could* be possible because they think about how your products are made all day long. But, sometimes, ideas are coming at you too fast and too often.

More complicated is when a senior leader comes to you with an idea. I call these "free ideas" – ironically – because, the truth is, they come at a cost. Or, more accurately, rejecting them comes at a cost. You can politely rebuff everyone else with an encouraging "great ideaaaa" or "we never thought of thatttt" in that high-pitched, super-impressed voice that we all use for not-a-great-idea-but-don't-want-to-hurt-your-feelings situations. But someone from the leadership team? They are your boss.

What is an innovator to do when you have an earnest senior leader who thinks they are a creative genius? Or, even worse, that their teenage son is? The problem is, even when their free ideas are good, they are probably a distraction. They aren't in the current pipeline, and they may or may not fit the current strategy. You need a robust but sensitive approach to deflect them.

A friend of mine had a great way of dealing with this. She devised a system of idea tickets for a particularly inventive boss. He got three per year, and he had to pull them off his wall and hand them in to her. At these moments, she would chase an idea, but no more often than that. This aggressive approach wouldn't work with all senior leaders, but this one had a good sense of humor, and he understood the need for boundaries.

My approach tends to be a bit gentler. I keep a list of all the free ideas I get from management. I will not drop everything and try to make them happen immediately, but I will include them in whatever concept screening process the team is doing as part of our annual innovation planning process. Sometimes, that means an idea stays parked on my "to test" list for months. But I keep track. And, occasionally, I've gotten a win-win-win where a free idea does fit our strategy, tests well, and comes to fruition, making that senior leader really proud.

But, remember, even though they're the boss, as the innovation owner, you are responsible for what ideas move forward.

When the free idea doesn't test well, I follow the same process I would with any other idea. But I don't go running back to the executive with an "I told you so" either. I just make sure I'm ready with a careful and clear response about the test results if the free idea is suggested again.

As the keeper of the innovation strategy, you must take charge and shut down distractions when necessary. It can be *very* frightening when the person you are shutting down signs your paycheck … or runs your company … or *owns* your company, but it's still your responsibility.

The challenge is, if you start taking free ideas because of the status of the person giving them, it's a slippery slope. I look at this in more detail in Chapter Thirteen. Your strategy can be pushed all over the place by fickle leaders distracted by short-term priorities or leaders so senior that they're not close enough to your work to understand the chaotic impact their suggestions could have. If they knew what you were up against every day, I'm sure they'd tell you to ignore their ideas.

So, find a respectful way to remind your creative leaders what the strategy and priorities are (often), and help them understand that free ideas can be costly. It's the only way to keep your team focused and your innovation engine on track.

And, finally, work on your high-pitched, super-impressed voice already. No one's buying it.

PART III:

LONG-TERM PLANNING

HOW TO BUILD AN INNOVATION PRACTICE THAT WILL LAST

CHAPTER TWELVE

NAILING INNOVATION PACING AND MIX

(reenter baseball analogy)

We've established that small ball wins baseball games. But then how do you explain the evil empire of the New York Yankees®? Good question. If you have the acquisition funding to *buy* winning new products rather than grow them yourself, great. Then you can be just like the Yankees, who buy talent other teams have built and play all-home-run baseball. And all your competitors will hate you.

Okay, I may have taken this baseball analogy one step too far (stupid Yankees).

Let's start over.

So, you want to build a smart portfolio investment approach to innovation? Don't we all?! It's not easy. How do you pick the right mix of projects you need to be successful long-term and pace them out in your calendar? How much innovation is enough? And how big should your ideas be? Innovation mix refers to the number of small, medium, and big bet projects you are working on. (If you've forgotten what I mean by small, medium, and big bet innovation, revisit the snack break before Chapter Three.)

To set the target for innovation pacing and mix on your business, start by evaluating your *internal and external innovation requirements*. Look at your category in terms of business growth, competitive edge, retail pressure, and innovation timelines.

Ask yourself these four questions:

1. How much growth are you trying to drive on the business in question?
Is it a high-growth business? If so, you will probably want innovation every year and more big innovations thrown into the mix. Is it a slow, steady-growth business, or a lower-priority business for you? If so, you will probably want innovation every other year, or even every three years, and mostly simple, smaller innovations.

2. How much competitive innovation is launching in your business's category?
I find it is often very helpful to look at the biggest and/or fastest-growing brands in my category and analyze how often they are innovating. If you want to keep up, you'll need to match their pace. If you want to lead, you'll need to beat it. You can look at this in terms of the number of items your competitors are launching or the amount of new revenue they are generating from those items. Either way, you can use their activity to set a target.

3. Are you getting pressure from your distributors, retailers, or operators for innovation? How often do they expect news?
I usually show a picture of Walmart® next to this question. If you work in consumer goods, you know why. Often, our internal team may be okay with less innovation, but our external customers – like Walmart –

are not. That's because they are under pressure to constantly grow the overall category and to justify the shelf space, warehouse slots, or truck space your products are taking up. That means there will always be a batch of products not performing that will be discontinued each year by retailers and/or distributors. This creates churn in the category, and the need to replace those items drives a need for innovation. You may be lucky enough to have a DTC (direct-to-consumer) model without any intermediates, and if so, this consideration won't apply. For the rest of us, think about what your role is in the category and whether there is an external expectation for a certain level of innovation. If you are a category leader, you are likely expected to bring innovation every year in order to replace your own items that are being discontinued.

4. What are the standard timelines in your business for innovation? How long does it take you to go from idea to market?
The answer could be six months ... or it could be six years. It could also vary based on how big the innovation is. If you are just getting started on an innovation pipeline, you may only be able to do a lot of *small* things in the short term. Big things need to be started well in advance because they usually require more development time, capital execution time, and consumer testing time.

Now you need to bring all this reflection together to create an ideal innovation calendar.

Try to fill in a three-year calendar matrix with your project slots, like the one below. If you work in areas where it takes six years to bring innovation to market, like many pharma or major technology categories, you need to extend this calendar out that many years versus the three I've shown.

What are project slots? They are the empty spaces where a project needs to go. I call them slots to highlight that they are empty because we don't know what the ideas are yet, and that's okay. We are trying to think through pacing *separately* from ideas. If you create an innovation calendar by just filling it with what you are already working on, you may not pace it out appropriately. This is about applying a strategy to your innovation timeline before innovation begins.

THREE-YEAR CALENDAR MATRIX SHOWING PROJECT SLOTS

	ONE YEAR OUT	TWO YEARS OUT	THREE YEARS OUT
SMALL, SUSTAINING INNOVATION	4 PROJECTS	4 PROJECTS	4 PROJECTS
MEDIUM INNOVATION	1 PROJECT		1 PROJECT
BIG BET INNOVATION		1 PROJECT	

In the example above, this innovator wants to launch something new and *big*. They know their lead time to market is two years, so they put that slot in year two (since they haven't started it yet). I've written that slot in gray to make it stand out to you because it is the anchor of this whole plan, and we will work our way up from our big bet. Since this example won't have big innovation until year two, in the meantime, the team will need something at least medium exciting next year and then again in three years when they are gearing up for another big innovation, presumably in year four.

However, those couple of items won't be enough to satisfy their big retail partners, so they have also added four small innovations to the plan for every year. This number was based on an analysis of how many of their own items are discontinued every year. This innovator estimates they need about five new things per year to maintain or grow their category share. If you add all the innovations up in each year, you'll see how they are able to deliver those five things.

Remember that you need a *mix* – small projects have their place.

The example above is pretty typical of what pacing and mix look like for a high-growth brand or category. Indeed, **I often see a <u>project mix</u> similar to:** 80% small, 15% medium, and 5% big bet innovation. Your <u>revenue mix</u> will be different and could skew higher toward big bets, given their size.

If you are looking at this mix and saying things like, "That's so much small stuff!" or, "Do we really want to have all that churn in our business?" or, "Why wouldn't we just do more big things?" remember my snack break *Fewer, Bigger, Better? Wrong. (Cut. It. Out.)*. This is a deeply flawed strategy. Yes, small innovation often only lasts in the market for 18-24 months. But small projects play an important role. In many categories, consumers are not brand loyal and can be attracted by the newest thing. These small innovations provide the news to keep your brand relevant and your consumers engaged with you. Brands with a lot of news are viewed as more modern; those without it are seen as sleepy. And in innovation, some churn is just part of life. Small innovation is usually necessary.

Critically, with our innovation calendar, we need to *start early*.

This is going to sound counterintuitive, but the advice I always give is that you need to **go slow to go fast.** The further in advance you are working on innovation, the easier it will be for you to pivot when necessary or to pull up a project if one fails in development (see Chapter Fifteen for more on pivoting). Having an innovation calendar that is scheduled for at least three years in advance is best in class.

The cliché you'll hear on this topic is "funnel not tunnel," implying it's better to have more ideas in the hopper, so that some can naturally fall out. Inexperienced innovation leaders will try to sell you on the idea that if you only work on the number of projects you *need*, you won't have enough that actually launch. **But in my 25+ year career, I've found the idea of an innovation funnel to be very unrealistic.** If I'm being honest, I think it's an example of something executives learn from consultants who don't live in the real world. Saying you will create a funnel implies you have the internal resources available to double, triple, or quadruple the work needed to launch a single innovation; and, on top of that, you will *plan* for the internal failure of most of those projects in the development phase, before they ever launch. Just to warn you, I'm going to rant now. First, very few organizations can afford to resource more projects than they need to launch. Second, if you work in an organization where everyone knows you don't *need* all of the projects you're developing, it creates a cancel culture. People look for reasons to throw a project out the window the moment things get hard rather than ways to pivot around project barriers. Innovation is always hard, so you can't give people a brightly-lit, easy-to-find emergency exit every time they get scared. It's a bit like suggesting you should have spare children. Horrifying idea, but it *is* a joke we told in my family of seven kids.

In contrast, a three-year pipeline does the work of the funnel … but it's more practical. That's because when you start projects sooner, you have both more information and more options. You know which projects in your pipeline are more likely to be "sure things" further in advance and which are riskier. If something fails during development, you can shuffle the chips on the board to fill the hole.

INNOVATION FUNNEL

AN UNREALISTIC IDEA THAT YOU CAN AFFORD TO START 4 PROJECTS AND ONLY LAUNCH 1 ON PURPOSE

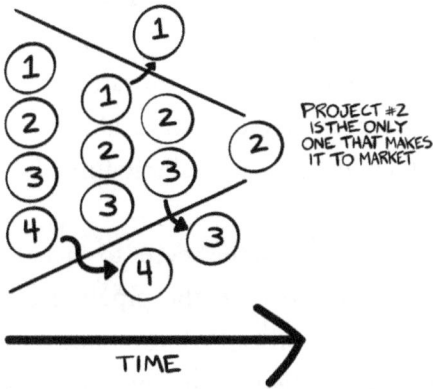

INNOVATION 3-YEAR CALENDAR

REALISTICALLY, SOME THINGS FAIL IN DEVELOPMENT, BUT YOU HAVE MORE COMING BEHIND THEM

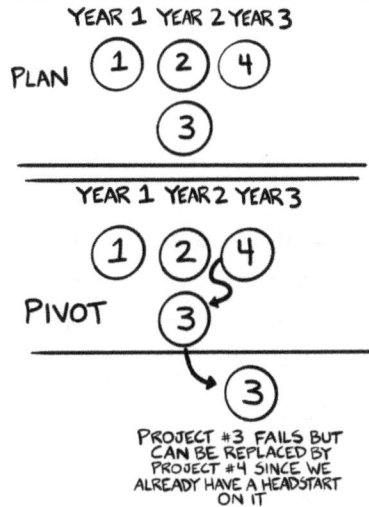

PROJECT #2 IS THE ONLY ONE THAT MAKES IT TO MARKET

TIME

YEAR 1 YEAR 2 YEAR 3

PLAN

YEAR 1 YEAR 2 YEAR 3

PIVOT

PROJECT #3 FAILS BUT CAN BE REPLACED BY PROJECT #4 SINCE WE ALREADY HAVE A HEADSTART ON IT

I want to be clear, I'm not anti-funnel because I want to work *fewer* innovation projects, although that might be one of the impacts of this choice. You'll remember from my snack break after Chapter Two I get nauseous when people say "fewer, bigger, better." But working on more projects *in a chaotic way*, where things are constantly cancelled, trains the wrong behaviors in the organization. It will keep you from getting the biggest and best ideas to market.

Knowing your spares helps too.

If you are running an effective innovation machine, once a year, you should test a big slug of ideas to populate the new third year of your calendar that is rolling into your plan. As part of that batch of ideas, I highly recommend making sure at least around 20% of them are things you have high confidence in your ability to execute. This doesn't mean they have to be small and dumb ideas. But you should have high confidence in your team's ability to execute them.

Then park those ideas as "spares" in your mind. Keep them in your pocket, and don't tell anyone about them; otherwise, they'll immediately become more attractive than the bigger, trickier ideas you've tasked people with producing. If people are working on projects with multiple barriers and they want to give up rather than pivot, they will look like a bright emergency exit sign. Don't add them onto your official project list, creating an unrealistic funnel.

In a real emergency, these spare projects can be the secret to success. When projects get off track and nothing else in the pipeline can move around, you'll need something to pull out of your hat on a now-crunched timeline. With an idea pulled from your spare list quickly, you'll look like the inspired innovation professional you are.

Now back to the calendar! Do your analysis, and create your slots timeline. Then you can start filling it in with projects. You'll soon be on your way to building a healthy innovation engine to drive growth for your company!

— *SNACK BREAK* —

INNOVATION CAN'T BE PAUSED

Executives must make trade-offs. I get that.

Something I've realized as I've advanced in my career is that when you are an individual-contributor-level employee, all you need to think about or advocate for is your own work. When you reach middle management, your primary job is to advocate for the work of your team, but you also need to understand the other priorities across the business and, sometimes, find compromises. Then you become an executive. (Good job!) Now you have to make the tough choices. There's no more doing the thing that's best for your function anymore. If a decision comes to you, someone usually has to win and someone has to lose. That means that, at times, people will hate you. But that's part of the job.

But when it comes to innovation, you can never pause it to resource something else. Innovation must always be an *and* to the other priorities in the business. It just takes too long to unpause.

Here are some typical executive comments that make me *furious*:

- **We can't focus on the long term right now; there are too many urgent short-term needs.**

    o *Um, yep, and there always will be if you have no long-term planning!*

- **We just need inexpensive, easy innovation right now; we can't invest in anything expensive.**
  - o *Then you will reap what you sow. It takes money to make money, so your incremental growth will be limited.*

- **We need to move resources off innovation and onto** *pick your priority* **(cost savings/renovation/capacity expansion) right now.**
  - o *You need to do all of that. Sounds like you need to develop the business case for incremental resources on either a temporary or permanent basis. All of those activities should pay back, and if you don't resource them all, you'll probably fail. Most businesses have to grow revenue AND profit, not one or the other.*

The problem with taking a break from innovation is the lead time involved in starting again.

Remember when we went through the innovation calendar, including how to pace each slot, and I said your first big project needs to be as many years out as your lead time for major innovation? That means if you stop, your next big innovation won't be next year. It might be two, three, or even six years out.

Innovation is like a giant ship. It turns slowly. In food and beverage categories, even when I'm running double time, I've found it takes at least one and a half years to develop a new pipeline from nothing … or from a pause, even if you carefully document everything you are currently working on, so you can pick it up again later. That practically never works because too much will have changed since the pause – the competition, the market, and the consumer will have kept evolving.

So, no, we can't take a break. Ever. Innovation can't be paused. I'm sorry, executives, but this is not an acceptable trade-off. Your job isn't just to make the *tough* call; it's also to make the *right* call. If you make the wrong one, you'll only be selling off the future.

INNOVATION STRATEGIES THAT RESIST THE WINDS OF CHANGE

Wait, you're thinking, *how is strategy writing (lucky) Chapter Thirteen? Surely, we should have <u>started</u> here. Doesn't strategy come first?* Well, you may be right. Strategy is at the beginning of everything, and without it, your innovation calendar will be a *random collection of crap.* *meaningful side eye*

But it can be a little overwhelming to write an innovation strategy from scratch. Now that we've talked about the innovation engine, how to pace it, and how to be creative, I think we are finally ready to tackle this head on … and I'm going to link all of those concepts together for you. You know how sometimes you get an email that is so long it really should have been a meeting? Well, this chapter should really be a workshop (and that is how I originally designed it). So buckle in. And while this chapter is another "how to," chances are, even if you are an experienced innovator, my approach will give you some new ideas.

An innovation strategy is really just about choices. Without one, you will succumb to what I call the **WINDS OF INNOVATION CHANGE.** They look something like this:

INTERNAL WINDS   EXTERNAL WINDS

YOUR COMPANY
CAPABILITIES

MANAGEMENT
PRIORITIES & "FREE
IDEAS"

YOUR
INNOVATION
STRATEGY

CUSTOMER/
DISTRIBUTOR
REQUESTS

CHANNEL NEEDS

BUSINESS
FINANCIAL NEEDS

CONSUMER TRENDS

SUPPLY CHAIN NEEDS
(E.G. AVAILABLE CAPACITY)

COMPETITIVE
ACTIONS

When you run innovation, everyone wants something from you. I'm still not sure whether this makes us popular … or just abused. In the absence of a strong strategy that you can use as protection to stand firm, you will get blown around … imagine these squiggly lines as gusts of wind and this strategy being blown all over the page!

For example, internally, you'll be encouraged to focus on your current company's technical capabilities (*blown downward*) or where there is available capacity in your operations/supply chain (*blown upward*). We talked about how management is always full of what I call "free ideas" – which is a nicer way of saying "bad ideas" – (*blown to the left*), and the owner of your P&L would *love* to make innovation the solution to their problem, whatever it is: likely that they need higher revenue or margins (*blown to the right*).

And those are just the friendly winds from your colleagues! Now think about all the demands from outside your company that you get from your customers or distribution partners, all the consumer trends you hear about and get asked to chase, plus the moves your competition makes that get everyone jumpy and wanting to respond in kind. At this point, you're being blown every which way.

Without an innovation strategy, in writing, that you remind everyone about at least once a year, you will struggle to stay upright and hold your ground.

So, you know you need one. Now let's talk about how to write one. There's no *one right way* to write an innovation strategy. The process below is my suggestion, which I've used across very different channels of business.

So, how should I write a category innovation strategy?

First, let me explain the name. I call it a category innovation strategy to distinguish it from a **project strategy**. Sometimes, teams write a strategy document for one big bet idea they want to pursue, so that everyone in the organization is clear on the objectives and parameters for it. There is a time and place for that, certainly, but what I'm outlining here is how to produce **an annual strategy for innovation across your entire category or business**. It should be part of the annual strategy planning work you do every year that leads to your target setting.

I also call it "category" because every category within your company should write its own innovation strategy. So, if you have a more complex business spanning across multiple categories, I recommend splitting them up for this work. Once you write a category strategy for each, you'll then need to create an overarching *company* strategy document that outlines your overall business objectives, the highest-priority categories for innovation, and (probably) what your high-level platforms and themes are for innovation across all businesses (note that the process below isn't for that either).

There are six steps you'll need to take if you want to build an effective innovation category strategy:

1. **Define your innovation target**
2. **Identify your focus areas**
3. **Determine your objectives**
4. **Create a calendar of projects (pacing)**
5. **Set your guardrails**
6. **Summarize your strategy, and use it to kick off your brainstorms**

If you want to follow along and work through these steps with your own business, you can find blank worksheets on my website, Innovationisugly.com.

STEP 1: DEFINE YOUR INNOVATION TARGET

Who is this innovation calendar for? There may be one group or several; it may the same people who buy your base business product or they could be different. If you work in innovation, you may think it's patronizing that I'm even talking to you about choosing a consumer target, but I place this first in the strategy document because it is one of the most important choices. While we tend to be good at clarifying who we are targeting on base businesses, we aren't always clear who our innovation is specifically for (often not the same people!). All innovation should be led by insights about what your consumer (if you are B2C) or customer (if you are B2B) needs. So, you need to know who that customer is before you do anything else. Ideally, each category should have one focused innovation target.

The innovation target should be the **group you believe your growth will come from.** So, if you don't know where to start, begin by doing some analysis of which demographics are growing fastest in your category or which ones are strong for your competitors but not for you. A lot of the time, this group ends up being younger or newer to the category than your base business users (but not always!).

Define your innovation target as thoroughly as you can against these four metrics:

1. **Who are they demographically?** What life stage are they in? Do they have kids? What age are they? How much money do they make? (For B2B, note that this may be more about where they are geographically and what business they operate in.)

2. **Who are they attitudinally?** What are their needs? What do they believe in? What are they struggling with?

3. **What are their behaviors?** How do they interact with your category? Are they heavy or light users? Do they buy a lot of variety or stay loyal to one part of the category? Where do they shop for your category, in terms of channels or stores? What else do they buy a lot of? What types of media do they consume (i.e., where would you advertise to them)?

4. **How do they feel about your products/brand?** While metrics one to three are about your target, this one is all about you. What are your strengths and opportunities with this target? What are their barriers to buying you?

Document all of this clearly, and make it accessible, so everyone who touches innovation can read it regularly and ensure it drives their decision-making. This will also help you to explain any choices you make on projects or ideas later on.

Here's an example of a fictional innovation target for a convenience store snack business.

CONVENIENCE STORE BROS

DEMOGRAPHICS:
- MOSTLY MALE
- 13-24 YEARS OLD
- URBAN CENTERS
- BLUE COLLAR WORKERS
- LOW-TO-MID INCOME

ATTITUDES:
- HATE "ADULTING"
- STRUGGLING FINANCIALLY
- ANXIOUS ABOUT FUTURE
- LOOKING FOR ESCAPE
- FRIENDS MOST IMPORTANT PEOPLE IN THEIR LIFE
- TOO YOUNG TO WORRY ABOUT NUTRITION OR CALORIES

BEHAVIORS:
- SHOP IN CONVENIENCE STORES 3+ TIMES A WEEK
- BUYING A LOT OF CAFFEINATED DRINKS, SALTY SNACKS, AND SWEET TREATS
- HEAVY VIDEO GAME USE
- HEAVY SOCIAL MEDIA USE
- LIMITED ON LINEAR TV OTHER THAN SPORTS
- EAT A LOT OF FOOD SERVICE MEALS, ESPECIALLY QUICK SERVICE

VIEW OF US:
- SEE OUR BRAND AS OUTDATED, "FOR OLD PEOPLE"
- WILL BUY US WHEN THERE ARE NO OTHER CHOICES
- ENJOY THE PRODUCT ONCE THEY'VE BOUGHT IT
- NEED TO GET THEM TO TRY US MORE OFTEN

STEP 2: IDENTIFY YOUR FOCUS AREAS

Now that you know the who, let's talk about the what. Answer the question: **Which part of our business are we going to innovate on?** You should have priorities, because you likely don't have the resources to innovate *everywhere*. This step is all about establishing clearly what those are.

In order to identify these priorities, first break your business into segments. These are different from categories (remember, this whole strategy document is for one category). Segments are more granular; it's about how your internal team, the customer, and the consumer would group the products in your category. They may be super obvious if your teams are already organized into groupings based on different parts of the business. If so, use those; that will be the cleanest approach. If not, I recommend thinking about how your business is organized operationally, how you report it financially, or how you bucket it for sales. The majority of the time, your segments are product types; for example, potato chips, pretzels, and tortilla chips are all in the salty snack category. "Clean," "moisture," and "for dyed hair" are different groupings of shampoos. If you don't have natural groupings based on product type, think about the different product lines you have and how they can logically be grouped by size, packaging type, format, channel, or price tier. There is no one way to approach this step; every category has its own segments that have developed over time.

Pro tip: As you are creating these segments, think about whether there are any *new ones* you want to add in your innovation calendar! For example, maybe you don't have any "moisture" offerings in your shampoo portfolio; this exercise might help you realize you want to add one.

Once you have your segments, rank order them based on how high of a priority innovation is for each. I find that this priority ranking is usually either exactly the same as how you are prioritizing those segments for investment already … or it's exactly the opposite of that. It may mirror your investment priorities because your core portfolio is the biggest and therefore exactly where you want the most innovation. Or it may be the opposite of your core investment priorities because the smallest part of your portfolio is actually the fastest growth space or has more white spaces for growth in the future.

Finally, choose a cutoff spot. You (probably) can't do innovation on *every* segment of your business. So, after you've put them in priority order, drop the last few … or the bottom half. Only *you* know what you can actually afford in terms of both people and financial resources. But a good rule I consider when deciding how many segments to prioritize is how high of a priority this *whole category* is to company growth. If you are a high-priority business, you'll probably be able to support more segments with innovation. If you are a low-priority one, you'll probably have very few to work with.

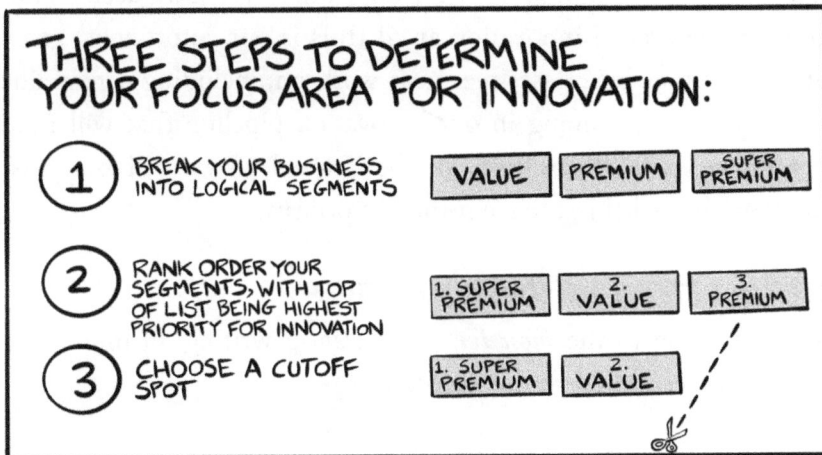

THREE STEPS TO DETERMINE YOUR FOCUS AREA FOR INNOVATION:

1. BREAK YOUR BUSINESS INTO LOGICAL SEGMENTS — VALUE | PREMIUM | SUPER PREMIUM

2. RANK ORDER YOUR SEGMENTS, WITH TOP OF LIST BEING HIGHEST PRIORITY FOR INNOVATION — 1. SUPER PREMIUM | 2. VALUE | 3. PREMIUM

3. CHOOSE A CUTOFF SPOT — 1. SUPER PREMIUM | 2. VALUE

Here's how this step of the strategy might play out for our convenience store snack business that is targeting "convenience store bros" (I'm using a worksheet format here that's available on innovationisugly.com).

PRIORITY ORDER	SEGMENTS OF OUR BUSINESS	HIGH PRIORITY FOR INNOVATION	LOW PRIORITY FOR INNOVATION	NO INNOVATION NEEDED
1	POTATO CHIPS	X		
3	TORTILLA CHIPS		X	
	PRETZELS			X
2	NEW: PUFFED SNACKS	X		

We have potato chips, tortilla chips, and pretzels in our fictional snacking company. Potato chips is the biggest part of our business and needs to be a high priority for innovation. We have decided not to prioritize pretzel innovation at all (this is our cutoff spot) given all of the other businesses we must work on, including a new line of puffed snacks coming in our innovation pipeline that will need ongoing news. Tortilla chips can't be ignored, so we will keep that segment on the list but make it the last priority.

STEP 3: DETERMINE YOUR OBJECTIVES

Now we come to the *most important step* in writing an innovation strategy: determining your objectives.

Objectives are the key outcome of your innovation strategy because they filter all the input you get from others down to simply what aligns with your goals. They provide a clear path forward.

INNOVATION STRATEGY ACTS AS A FILTER FOR THE WINDS OF INNOVATION CHANGE

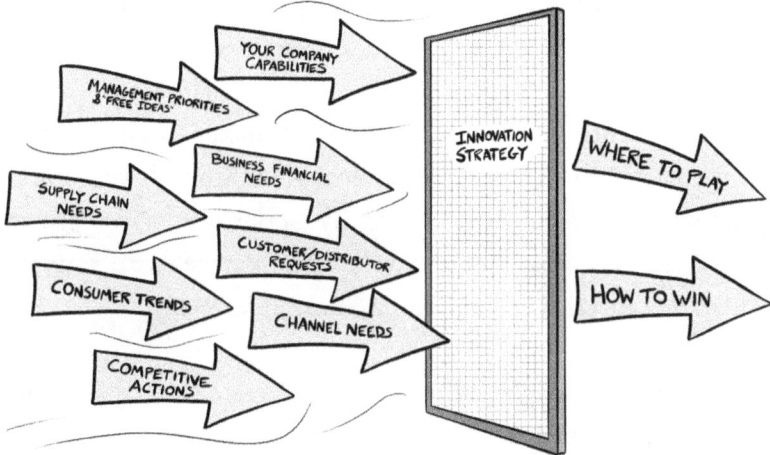

You will write *at least one objective* for each of your prioritized focus areas. If they are high priority, you might have two or even three objectives (you should not be writing objectives tied to focus areas you deprioritized).

Objectives are single sentences that answer two questions: **WHERE do we want to play, and HOW will we win in that space?**

Let's talk about **where to play** first. This should be based on how your business breaks down consumer usage. How do you think about all the cases where someone might use your product? Some teams refer to these as innovation "jobs," some call them occasions, some just call them growth territories. How have *you* organized those use cases to sort them and find the biggest growth opportunities?

You may have sorted your product uses by:
- occasions (times of day or times of year)
- needs (what a product does for a consumer)
- channels (where your product is purchased)

- location (where your product is used, like at home vs. in car vs. at school)
- target consumers (if you have more than one innovation target, you may want to organize uses by your targets)

Once you've chosen whatever framework makes the most sense for your use cases, list the top-priority spaces within it. If you don't have a framework that you use to identify opportunities for growth in product use cases, you should develop one! Partner with your friends in consumer insights or analytics to make it happen.

Here are some examples from our convenience store snack business case study. The fictional innovators on this business decided occasions were the best way to organize use cases. They've picked some of the biggest, fastest-growing occasions in snacking for our target consumer to focus on for their innovation:

- Morning on-the-way-to-work snacking
- Weekend road trip snacking
- After-work evening snacking
- Packed lunch snacks (for those packing lunch for work or high school/college)

Looking at your use cases will tell you **where to play.**

I recommend including both the territory and your goal when you write your where to play statement down. It may be as simple as grow sales in this territory, but it sometimes is about penetration, premium price tier expansion, or some other business goal. Make sure you include that in your objective.

Now, to finish writing the objective, you need to add your own *specific* thinking on **how to win** in those use cases. The important part of that sentence was *specific*. Be very clear on what it will take to win each usage opportunity. Your **how to win** will be based on your knowledge of consumer insights, trends, and your own capabilities, so I can't really counsel you on this. But I will show you some strong examples of objectives that pair **how to win** statements with **where to play** choices.

Example objectives for our convenience store snack business:

INNOVATION OBJECTIVES

WHERE TO PLAY	HOW TO WIN	THREE TO FIVE WORD SUMMARY
GROW SALES IN MORNING ON-THE-WAY-TO-WORK OCCASION...	...BY INTRODUCING POTATO CHIP SNACK FLAVORS THAT GO WELL WITH THE COFFEE CONSUMERS ARE DRINKING IN THE CAR.	POTATO CHIP COFFEE PAIRINGS
EXPAND OUR WEEKEND ROAD TRIP ASSORTMENT...	...BY CREATING PUFFED SNACK FORMS WITH A CRUNCH THAT KEEPS ME ALERT WHILE DRIVING.	EXTREME CRUNCH PUFFED SNACKS
EXPAND OUR USAGE OCCASIONS AFTER WORK...	...BY CREATING MORE INDULGENT PUFFED SNACKS.	MORE INDULGENT PUFFED SNACKS
INCREASE OUR LOW PENETRATION IN PACKED LUNCHES...	...WITH ENGAGING TORTILLA CHIP SNACK KITS THAT PROVIDE AN ALL-IN-ONE LUNCH OPTION THAT COMPETE WITH FROZEN MEALS AND SANDWICHES.	TORTILLA CHIP LUNCH KITS

When you read the objectives above, you'll notice that the **how to win** parts of each objective aren't just pulled out of the air. They imply that a lot of analysis and learning has been done to identify the growth opportunities and needs of consumers in these use cases. If you don't have that depth of learning, you'll struggle to write strong innovation objectives, so this must be part of your process.

In the example above, we've written more than one objective for puffed snacks because we are really looking to expand in that space in a big way. Even though potato chips are our number-one priority, the innovation in that space is pretty simple (flavors). Is this what you were imagining when you thought about innovation for potato chips, puffed snacks, and tortilla chips a few pages ago? Probably not. Now the innovations are really starting to crystalize in our minds. Without this clear process to guide us, we might have created innovation that was completely different from what the business needs to win. And that is the reason why these objectives matter so much. **They will provide the brief for your innovation brainstorm and drive your innovation calendar,** so you must give them the attention they need.

You'll also notice that I added a third column in the table with a quick three- to five-word summary of the objective. This is a useful shorthand we can use internally when we talk about these strategic objectives.

Some watchouts for you; I often find these mistakes are made in innovation objectives:

1. **They aren't specific enough.** Be specific about the use case you are targeting and what you know about the needs/insights for that case. Be specific about the business goal too. All innovation is designed to grow the business, so add a metric that makes it clear in what way it will do so.

2. **Your "where to play" focuses on the business objective and not the innovation objective.** I see strategies all the time that are about growing the base business using innovation. Or about solving a base business problem. Innovation doesn't do that (see the snack break between Chapters One and Two).

3. **You write your objectives in business-speak, with tons of acronyms and inside terminology.** This is a mistake because the entire business team needs to easily understand your strategy. Great strategies can be summarized in a couple of words.

STEP 4: CREATE A CALENDAR OF PROJECTS (PACING)

The good news is, you already know all about this! We discussed pacing in Chapter Twelve. If you need a refresher, feel free to flip back. If you recall, the outcome of a pacing exercise is a three-year calendar of "slots" – holes where projects go. Now that we have our focus areas and objectives, we can make these slots even more specific.

Here's the calendar for our convenience store snack business based on the strategy we've written so far. We need a minimum of two projects per year to keep up with the competition.

CONVENIENCE STORE SNACKS 3 YEAR INNOVATION PACING CALENDAR

	ONE YEAR OUT	TWO YEARS OUT	THREE YEARS OUT
SMALL, SUSTAINING INNOVATION	POTATO CHIP COFFEE PAIRING FLAVORS (1 PROJECT)		
MEDIUM INNOVATION		MORE INDULGENT PUFFED SNACKS (2 PROJECTS)	EXTREME CRUNCH PUFFED SNACKS (1 FLAVOR EXPANSION PROJECT)
BIG BET INNOVATION	EXTREME CRUNCH PUFFED SNACKS (1 PROJECT)		TORTILLA CHIP LUNCH KITS (1 PROJECT)

STEP 5: SET GUARDRAILS

Remember how we talked in Chapter Six about how creativity needs guardrails?

A great next step to take as part of your annual strategy is to align your key stakeholders on your guardrails for any new innovation ideation. This keeps everyone focused on exactly what is needed to succeed in your category. Guardrails need to consider ALL aspects of your proposition.

You may have different guardrails for each segment of your business, or they may all be the same for your category in total.

I find when writing guardrails, it helps to use a framework to make sure you aren't missing anything. I've created one below that is an adaptation of the 4 Ps of marketing (originally created in 1960 by E. Jerome McCarthy, a marketing professor). I've filled in examples of guardrails you might consider along each dimension of an innovation. You can use this example and customize the areas that make the most sense for your own category.

PRODUCT	PACKAGING	PLACE	PRICE/PACKAGE ARCHITECTURE	TECHNOLOGY BENEFIT
• SHAPE/FORM • SIZE • APPEARANCE • CATEGORY • FLAVOR • INGREDIENTS, COMPONENTS, MATERIALS • NAME/BRANDING	• SHAPE • SIZE/COUNT • MATERIAL • OPENING FEATURE • RECLOSING FEATURE • TRANSFORMATION CAPABILITY	• DISTRIBUTION CHANNEL TARGETED • PART OF STORE • TEMPERATURE STATE (FROZEN, REFRIGERATED, SHELF STABLE)	• VALUE/PRICE • SIZE FLEXIBILITY TO HIT PRICE POINTS	• CLAIMS • COMPETITIVE ADVANTAGES • CAPABILITIES • NEW INGREDIENTS OR COMPONENTS

Once you have your universe of guardrails to consider, there are three essential questions you need to answer in order to identify the guardrails most critical for you. These address what *cannot* change, what *can* change, and what new *technologies* are desired.

WHAT ELEMENTS ARE CRITICAL TO OUR BRAND POSITIONING OR CATEGORY STRATEGY AND MUST BE MAINTAINED?

WHAT ELEMENTS CAN CHANGE AND SHOULD THEREFORE BE THE FOCUS OF INNOVATION?

WHAT NEW PRODUCT AND PACKAGING TECHNOLOGIES SHOULD R & D FOCUS ON THAT WILL ALLOW US TO DELIVER ON OUR INNOVATION OBJECTIVES?

CRITICAL ELEMENTS TO MAINTAIN

ELEMENTS OPEN TO CHANGE

NEW PRODUCT & PACKAGE TECHNOLOGIES DESIRED

Let's explore each of these in more detail.

1. What elements are critical to our brand positioning or category strategy and must be maintained?

This is really a summary of your brand/product offering's key elements. These are the parts of the offering that drive the benefit or point of difference that allow you to stand out from the competition. As a starting point, you need to know what actually matters to consumers. I often find that marketers and R&D folks will put more elements on this list as guardrails than necessary, so watch out for that tendency. That happens partly because we sometimes think consumers have a narrower view of how far our brands can stretch than they do and partly because we sometimes focus only on our existing manufacturing or service capabilities. Remember that innovation projects *can* invest in new capabilities beyond what you are able to make today, so these guardrails should not *just* describe your current offerings in detail. However, if you know there are capabilities that aren't affordable or that you need to work within certain manufacturing constraints, you *should* list those here.

Let's say I'm writing guardrails for our convenience store snack business. I might include things like this:

```
┌─────────────────────────────┐
│  CRITICAL ELEMENTS          │
│     TO MAINTAIN             │
├─────────────────────────────┤
│ · CRISPY WITH A LIGHT       │
│   CRUNCH (THIS IS CORE      │
│   TO OUR EQUITY)            │
│                             │
│ · NATURAL SHAPES LIKE       │
│   ROUND AND TRIANGLE        │
│   (CONSUMER LEARNING        │
│    INDICATES UNNATURAL      │
│    SHAPES MAKE THEM         │
│    THINK THE PRODUCT        │
│    IS OVERLY MANUFACTURED)  │
│                             │
│ · SALTY OR SPICY FLAVOR     │
│   PROFILE (THESE BRANDS     │
│   DON'T STAND FOR SWEET)    │
│                             │
│ · PACKED IN PILLOW POUCH    │
│   BAGS (THAT'S OUR ONLY     │
│   PACKAGING CAPABILITY,     │
│   AND NEW PACKAGING         │
│   EQUIPMENT IS TOO          │
│   EXPENSIVE FOR             │
│   INNOVATION TO AFFORD)     │
│                             │
│ · SHELF STABLE (WE DON'T    │
│   HAVE DISTRIBUTION FOR     │
│   FROZEN OR REFRIGERATED    │
│   ITEMS)                    │
└─────────────────────────────┘
```

2. What elements can CHANGE and should therefore be the focus of innovation?

You may not be able to imagine all the possibilities here because this is really the focus of what the innovation will deliver! That's okay. Some new things may come out of ideations and will have to be added later. I usually encourage innovators to focus on the *most debatable* product features in this section, meaning those elements that you can argue are either critical or not critical to keep, depending on your perspective. This is your chance to clarify if the innovation team can look at some of those things ... or not. This section should *not* read like the opposite of the "critical elements to maintain" section. That would be a silly waste of time. It should list different elements.

Here's an example for our convenience store snack business:

```
┌─────────────────────────────┐
│   ELEMENTS OPEN             │
│     TO CHANGE               │
├─────────────────────────────┤
│ · MULTITEXTURE              │
│   SNACKS (AS LONG AS         │
│   CRUNCH IS ONE OF           │
│   THE TEXTURES)              │
│                             │
│ · NEW GRAINS,               │
│   ESPECIALLY HIGH            │
│   FIBER ONES                 │
│                             │
│ · PACKAGING KITS            │
│   COMBINING POUCHED          │
│   SNACKS WITH HIGH           │
│   PROTEIN DIPS AND/          │
│   OR TOPPINGS                │
│                             │
│ · PACKAGING SIZING—         │
│   MULTI-SERVE, SINGLE        │
│   SERVE                      │
│                             │
└─────────────────────────────┘
```

In this example, my fictional team has been debating multitexture and use of alternative grains, so the innovator has called them out here and gained alignment from the team to pursue that type of innovation.

3. **What new product and packaging technologies should R&D focus on that will allow us to deliver on our innovation objectives?**

This last question is really about specific elements you want to *add* to your product lineup but don't have the solutions for yet. Guardrails are about steering. what you want to move your team toward and away from. Desired technologies are a clear signal to your technical team that you want research done or suppliers identified in these spaces. Typically, these desired technologies will come to mind when you are writing your objectives. For example, our fictional convenience store innovator wants to ideate new potato chip flavors for pairing with coffee. Maybe they want some of those flavors to have a caffeine benefit, but they don't know how to deliver that. They are also frustrated because they know young guys would love nacho kits for lunch with meat-based dips, but the team has never found a solution that is both affordable and would have a long enough expiration date on it. Finally, they would *love* to be able to deliver multitexture snacks that are crunchy on the outside and soft on the inside! They've never been able to figure this out so far, but they know, from previous consumer research, that it's a *big idea*. All of these desired technologies and benefits show up in our guardrail table.

DESIRED TECHNOLOGIES
• CAFFEINE TECHNOLOGY AND INGREDIENTS
• HIGH PROTEIN DIPS, IDEALLY INCLUDING MEAT
• ABILITY TO ADD SOFT FILLING TO PUFFED SNACKS (E.G. PEANUT BUTTER)

And now your guardrails are complete!

GUARDRAILS

CRITICAL ELEMENTS TO MAINTAIN	ELEMENTS OPEN TO CHANGE	DESIRED TECHNOLOGIES
• CRISPY WITH A LIGHT CRUNCH • NATURAL SHAPES LIKE ROUND AND TRIANGLE • SALTY OR SPICY FLAVOR PROFILE • PACKED IN PILLOW POUCH BAGS • SHELF STABLE	• MULTITEXTURE SNACKS (AS LONG AS CRUNCH IS ONE OF THE TEXTURES) • NEW GRAINS, ESPECIALLY HIGH FIBER ONES • PACKAGING KITS COMBINING POUCHED SNACKS WITH HIGH PROTEIN DIPS AND/OR TOPPINGS • PACKAGING SIZING — MULTI-SERVE, SINGLE SERVE	• CAFFEINE TECHNOLOGY AND INGREDIENTS • HIGH PROTEIN DIPS, IDEALLY INCLUDING MEAT • ABILITY TO ADD SOFT FILLING TO PUFFED SNACKS (E.G. PEANUT BUTTER)

STEP 6: SUMMARIZE YOUR STRATEGY, AND USE IT TO KICK OFF YOUR BRAINSTORMS

Once you have workshopped through each of these steps, you need to summarize the output in one place. I don't usually include the focus areas worksheet in my summary. It is a helpful exercise as a lead-in to writing objectives, but it only needs to be shared out broadly if you think there will be debate about which businesses are supported by innovation. (I have worked on teams where that was the case, and the focus areas had to be shared out not only once a year, but *every month*, or my team would get requests to support categories we had deprioritized.)

Create a simple summary of your innovation strategy, with the key components, and share this broadly with your leadership team and key stakeholders across the business. Remember that an innovation strategy needs to be clear and well understood by *everyone* who touches innovation in your company. It should be simple enough to be easily explainable to stakeholders, including the board of directors, Wall Street investors, customers, and suppliers.

Whoa, that was a LOT. Take a breath.

In case you've forgotten, here are the six steps again.
1. Define your innovation target
2. Identify your focus areas
3. Determine your objectives
4. Create a calendar of projects (pacing)
5. Set guardrails
6. Summarize your strategy, and use it to kick off your brainstorms

Now you know WHO you are innovating for, WHAT segments you are innovating in, WHERE TO PLAY (your usages) and HOW TO WIN within those segments, HOW OFTEN you will innovate, and the GUARDRAILS for your ideation. Amazing!

With all of these to hang on to, *no one* can blow you off your feet again, right!?? This armor will help you defend against the windbags.

Summary of Innovation Strategy Workshop Outputs

CONVENIENCE STORE BROS

DEMOGRAPHICS:
- MOSTLY MALE
- 13-24 YEARS OLD
- URBAN CENTERS
- BLUE COLLAR WORKERS
- LOW-TO-MID INCOME

ATTITUDES:
- HATE "ADULTING"
- STRUGGLING FINANCIALLY
- ANXIOUS ABOUT FUTURE
- LOOKING FOR ESCAPE
- FRIENDS MOST IMPORTANT PEOPLE IN THEIR LIFE
- TOO YOUNG TO WORRY ABOUT NUTRITION OR CALORIES

BEHAVIORS:
- SHOP IN CONVENIENCE STORES 3+ TIMES A WEEK
- BUYING A LOT OF CAFFEINATED DRINKS, SALTY SNACKS, AND SWEET TREATS
- HEAVY VIDEO GAME USE
- HEAVY SOCIAL MEDIA USE
- LIMITED ON LINEAR TV OTHER THAN SPORTS
- EAT A LOT OF FOOD SERVICE MEALS, ESPECIALLY QUICK SERVICE

VIEW OF US:
- SEE OUR BRAND AS OUTDATED, "FOR OLD PEOPLE"
- WILL BUY US WHEN THERE ARE NO OTHER CHOICES
- ENJOY THE PRODUCT ONCE THEY'VE BOUGHT IT
- NEED TO GET THEM TO TRY US MORE OFTEN

INNOVATION OBJECTIVES

WHERE TO PLAY	HOW TO WIN	THREE TO FIVE WORD SUMMARY
GROW SALES IN MORNING ON-THE-WAY-TO-WORK OCCASION...	...BY INTRODUCING POTATO CHIP SNACK FLAVORS THAT GO WELL WITH THE COFFEE CONSUMERS ARE DRINKING IN THE CAR.	POTATO CHIP COFFEE PAIRINGS
EXPAND OUR WEEKEND ROAD TRIP ASSORTMENT...	...BY CREATING PUFFED SNACK FORMS WITH A CRUNCH THAT KEEPS ME ALERT WHILE DRIVING.	EXTREME CRUNCH PUFFED SNACKS
EXPAND OUR USAGE OCCASIONS AFTER WORK...	...BY CREATING MORE INDULGENT PUFFED SNACKS.	MORE INDULGENT PUFFED SNACKS
INCREASE OUR LOW PENETRATION IN PACKED LUNCHES...	...WITH ENGAGING TORTILLA CHIP SNACK KITS THAT PROVIDE AN ALL-IN-ONE LUNCH OPTION THAT COMPETE WITH FROZEN MEALS AND SANDWICHES.	TORTILLA CHIP LUNCH KITS

GUARDRAILS

CRITICAL ELEMENTS TO MAINTAIN	ELEMENTS OPEN TO CHANGE	DESIRED TECHNOLOGIES
- CRISPY WITH A LIGHT CRUNCH - NATURAL SHAPES LIKE ROUND AND TRIANGLE - SALTY OR SPICY FLAVOR PROFILE - PACKED IN PILLOW POUCH BAGS - SHELF STABLE	- MULTI-TEXTURE SNACKS (AS LONG AS CRUNCH IS ONE OF THE TEXTURES) - NEW GRAINS, ESPECIALLY HIGH FIBER ONES - PACKAGING KITS COMBINING POUCHED SNACKS WITH HIGH PROTEIN DIPS AND/OR TOPPINGS - PACKAGING SIZING — MULTI-SERVE, SINGLE SERVE	- CAFFEINE TECHNOLOGY AND INGREDIENTS - HIGH PROTEIN DIPS, IDEALLY INCLUDING MEAT - ABILITY TO ADD SOFT FILLING TO PUFFED SNACKS (I.E. PEANUT BUTTER)

CONVENIENCE STORE SNACKS 3 YEAR INNOVATION PACING CALENDAR

	ONE YEAR OUT	TWO YEARS OUT	THREE YEARS OUT
SMALL, SUSTAINING INNOVATION	POTATO CHIP COFFEE PAIRING FLAVORS (1 PROJECT)		
MEDIUM INNOVATION		MORE INDULGENT PUFFED SNACKS (2 PROJECTS)	EXTREME CRUNCH PUFFED SNACKS (1 FLAVOR EXPANSION PROJECT)
BIG BET INNOVATION	EXTREME CRUNCH PUFFED SNACKS (1 PROJECT)		TORTILLA CHIP LUNCH KITS (1 PROJECT)

— *SNACK BREAK* —

THE GAP-CLOSER MERRY-GO-ROUND

Well, that chapter on strategy was the *longest* in the book so far. You might have read it and thought ... NAAAAAHHHHH. It sounded too hard. Too complicated. Like a bunch of theoretical hoo-ha that had nothing to do with reality.

Unfortunately, I can tell you from ugly experience what happens when you don't have a clear strategy and a long-term pacing calendar developed. You get on the gap-closer merry-go-round (it isn't merry, though; it's actually really shitty).

The truth is, if you don't have a long-term strategy, you will *never* focus on the future. Sure, you'll talk about it. But it will always be just out of reach ... because you have to deliver *this year's* plan. You need something to present to a customer next month! Do you know how many times I've seen teams *start* ideating next year's innovation *after* that major customer annual review is scheduled? *face palm* This is what happens without a long-term plan; you are just scrambling to come up with this year's plan all the time. And you are always too far behind to think about what could be next.

Then, one year, your business is off track and behind plan; as the innovator, you are being asked to fix that. You are probably being told you must deliver a specific number of new items or an amount of innovation revenue to close the gap in the plan. And because that gap must be closed *immediately*, you probably won't be able to do something that delivers against your innovation objectives. You should have written them (and a pacing calendar) sooner!

Nope, you'll just have to launch something that fits your urgent timeline. And what fits the timeline? Something that already exists, probably because it failed once before. Or something that is really easy to do, probably because it's very similar to what you already do. Only small stuff is fast. And, remember, small stuff is okay when it's in a mix of medium and big bet projects. But small stuff is usually less incremental to the business, so your innovation isn't going to be driving real growth.

You are just going in circles. You are frantically launching things to replace the things you launched two years ago that aren't working. And you can't ever get ahead … because you are always behind.

Get off the shit-go-round (it's not merry).

Write a long-term innovation strategy and stick to it.

CHAPTER FOURTEEN

STOP YAMMERING ABOUT "TRENDS"

The word "innovation" often gets wrapped up in people's minds with the idea of trends. I'm going to take an unpopular point of view in this chapter: I don't think innovators need to pay *nearly* as much attention to trends as executives think they do.

When I used to run innovation strategy, one of my annual tasks was to update the view of long-term trends for the company. For that purpose, I would bring together all the innovation leaders across the company; we would discuss all the top trends and then narrow them down to the four or five most critical ones. After a few years of doing this exercise, I had one of those *aha* moments that feel like a real epiphany at the time but, later, seem blatantly obvious.

1.   Long-term trends *don't change over the short term.*
2.   Short-term trends *don't make for long-term innovation.*

What I mean is that the "trends" we were talking about each year were things all of us had been tracking for *years* already. It was silly to document them like they were new information. The reality is, consumer behavior usually changes pretty slowly, absent some major disruption. That's why it's often expressed as an adoption cycle. Adoption cycles look like a hill with a long lead-up; that means they have a slow build at the beginning followed by a big hump when the majority of people make a shift toward a certain consumer behavior.

TREND ADOPTION CYCLE

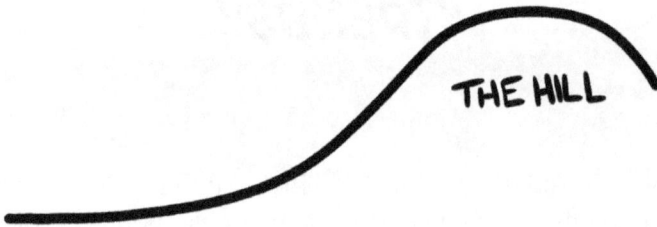

THE HILL

That long, slow plateau before the hill is why I'm telling you to stop yammering about short-term trends. A lot of things hang out in that "new and hip" space for a while. You'll see consumer behavior showing it's becoming popular, but it'll mostly be among celebrities or in niche shops or trendy coastal cities or only in the service industry. Depending on the pace of innovation in your category, "new and hip" could last six months or 10 years. And not all things make it up the hill; in fact, many don't. The truth is, "new and hip" trends usually test terribly with the broader population. They are still too weird. And they might just be blips on the radar, never turning into a long-term bet.

Until a trend starts to climb the hill, I recommend only doing exploratory work around the space and not committing any resources to it.

TREND ADOPTION CYCLE

"THAT'S OVER"

"NEW AND HIP"   "EVERYONE'S
                        DOING IT!"

I will give you an example from the food industry: gluten free products (I know it's a dietary restriction for some people who have a horrible disease, but it's also a trend). As an innovator, gluten free showed up on my radar as a trend somewhere around 2008. It didn't really take off and get broader attention from consumers until around 2010, and at that point, a lot of them still couldn't (correctly) tell you what "gluten" was. Some just said it was "bad." Mondelez didn't launch the gluten free Oreo® until 2021. Today, gluten free is still a somewhat niche idea, and it's still considered a trend after more than 15 years. I would say it's probably still on its way up the hill. That's how slowly a change in consumer behavior can unfold.

Shifting to eating more real, whole foods has been a trend in food for almost my entire career. Making things easier and more convenient is also a trend in almost every category that uses innovation; we just keep changing what "convenient" means to us.

As you can see, long-term trends don't change fast. Indeed, they are foundational – driving some of the consumer needs or barriers for your category, so they should be the backbone of your strategy, informing those objectives we wrote back in Chapter Twelve.

For this reason, it's important that you know them *inside out* – acknowledge them, document them, and then focus on breaking down the barriers to solving these evergreen challenges. If you can't articulate four to five long-term trends driving innovation in your space, you're in trouble. So, do your homework with your insights/analytics partners, with syndicated research, and with your consumers. Use them to focus on the future and not the present – that way, you can't get bogged down in fads.

Despite all this, I am a sucker for an annual trend tour.

I always incorporate these as part of the ideation process for the calendar-year-three ideas we are adding each year. Go to markets with lots of your category's early adopters (read: young people, normally). And visit stores or services that are local, niche, and doing risky things. Sure, it's fun, but this isn't about being swayed by what's in fashion; my epiphany above still holds. Most of the time, you will just reinforce what you already know to be the trends in your category. But remember that a lot of creativity in innovation comes from *how* you solve the category problems. And seeing different solutions and approaches may just inspire your team.

What about fads?

In today's fast-paced world of social media content creators, there are a lot more fast-cycle fads. These may only last a month, a week, or a few days. And when your CEO's teenage son forwards a trend to her, you are going to get asked to jump on it.

Having read this chapter, I'm sure you think I'd recommend giving that CEO a withering look. But there is a place for fads (don't look so shocked).

Fads are temporary, by definition, but if you have a business model that allows you to launch something before your consumer loses interest, go for it! Be agile! But don't invest big here. Chasing fads is a way to develop quick, small ideas for your close-in pipeline.

You can also create the fads yourself with the right investments. Find the right partner (an influencer, retailer, PR agency, or celebrity) and make something go viral for a short time. This is really a marketing stunt with an innovation assist, but it can make your brand feel more relevant and win you some publicity. For brands targeting younger consumers especially, this can go a long way in building your equity.

To sum up, if you are a good innovator, you *know* your long-term trends, and you shouldn't focus on short-term trends unless you have a strategy to chase fads. So, reassure your executives that you aren't missing anything.

— *SNACK BREAK* —

BUILDING VS. BUYING INNOVATION

At a corporate level, there are two ways to drive growth through new items – you can build them, or you can buy them. There are real advantages to both. This may seem like a surprising point of view coming from a lifelong innovator (and a "team build" badge wearer), but remember that the best creative ideas are usually obvious. If so, there's a chance they are already being done. By someone else. But probably on a small scale. **So, go find that small business, buy it, and scale it up!**

Use the "buy" strategy in partnership with your innovation "build" strategy.
- **Buy things you know you can't do yourself.** This is a great way to produce breakthrough innovation without all the up-front risk and capital investment. Good "buy" targets have manufacturing assets you need, technical know-how you don't have, and a believable chance at scale with your investment behind them (for example, if they're being handmade, this may not be a feasible opportunity, as you'll have to invest a *lot* to scale them up).
- **Have strategy and innovation leaders collaborate to produce an opportunity map.** This is a mind map visual that charts out all of the biggest areas of expansion for the build team

(innovation) and the buy team (mergers and acquisitions). Aligning on a more holistic plan can be a really smart way to maximize growth.

- **Add an innovation expert to your acquisitions team.** They will have the experience and gut instincts to know how big something could be or how hard it might be to scale. It will also keep you from overlapping in your investments – your acquisitions team may be looking at things you are already building internally, for instance.

- **Fund startups that have great ideas but need capital.** Get a stake in a tiny business doing something you wish you could in case it's one of the unicorns that actually succeeds. A large amount of money to them is probably a small amount to you.

But when should you stick with the build strategy?

When you do the math on build vs. buy (and I've done it, in great detail), build usually wins, and often by a lot of moolah. Even accounting for all of the capital required to build and all of the marketing to create a new brand, if that's necessary. Buying something really just reduces the risk of initial failure, but for a very high price. The multiples required to buy more established small businesses in the U.S. today are *high* – often well north of the typical three to five times the annual earnings of a company.

If you have an innovation engine with a track record of success, you may not need as many acquisitions. You may be able to drive consistent organic growth instead. In that scenario, innovation will start to look a lot less ugly than the expensive alternative.

CHAPTER FIFTEEN

PIVOT AROUND BARRIERS

Sometimes, I look at a room in my house and I'm hit with inspiration. I start imagining how to fit the same things into that square space but just … differently. What can I say. I'm in innovation. I like rearranging furniture. It changes the way I see a room and how I use it. Lots of ideas usually start popping into my head at the same time. *What if I put the shelf in front of the window? What if I moved the sofa into the middle of the room?*

The problem is, my imagination is never quite to scale (and I don't believe in measuring before rearranging … because where's the fun in that?!). So, I will start moving everything around all at once, and I usually end up with most of it in the middle of the room, at wild angles, stuck. Stuck on the rug (which is now bunched up). Stuck in one corner of the room without enough leeway to turn any further. Or stuck wedged behind a table. My vision for how things will come together beautifully has to be reimagined. I have to take a different path … maybe even accept a slightly different outcome. I'm not ready to give up, but I've got to find a way to pivot that dang giant shelf around the table!

This chaotic picture is a good analogy for a typical innovation project. At the beginning of an innovation journey, you may suspect *something* will go wrong, but it's often difficult to predict what that something will be. Because you're doing something *new*, you can't always guess correctly how the pieces will come together. Everyone starts working on their different parts and, suddenly, you find yourselves stuck. All bunched up. Remember, innovation is hard! We talked in Chapter One about the many modes of failure. You need a strong stomach to be an innovator, because if you want to be successful, it's probably going to be a twisty, turny ride. But you can't give up. You need to find a way to pivot the pieces of the project to slide past the obstacles in your path.

If you get stuck, *keep pivoting*, and don't give up.

If you want to launch big innovation especially, know that problems *will* come up, and you are going to have to be flexible. Your job as an innovator is to know what parts of the project can flex and which are dealbreakers. The good news is that having to pivot can enrich the project. I find that the most valuable creativity in the innovation process comes from finding ways around barriers that appear immovable.

If you are stuck, go back to your innovation guardrails (that we discussed in Chapter Thirteen). Can any of the innovation's elements change?

PRODUCT	PACKAGING	PLACE	PRICE/PACKAGE ARCHITECTURE	TECHNOLOGY BENEFIT

Can you reimagine the product in a different form? Can it be packaged in a new, unexpected way? If you can't make it work for one channel, would it be great for another? Does it need to be priced or sized differently to deliver value? If you can't deliver on the intended benefit, is there anything you could deliver instead that consumers would be excited about? If it's too costly to buy the manufacturing equipment needed, can a contract manufacturer make it for you initially (then, if it works, you could still invest in that equipment!).

Your best friend in consumer insights will need to be by your side to make sure any pivots you make don't shift you away from the consumer need you are trying to deliver on. But I find that problems usually arise for internal reasons. We can't make something at all, or we can't make it affordably.

It's so important not to give up the first time a part of your innovation project hits a wall. One way to approach pivoting is to have a pilot facility where you can play with changes to the product concept. It allows for a much greater number of scale trials, which will dramatically increase your success. Keep trying different approaches until you find a solution.

Finally, know who to put in charge of pivoting. Surprise, surprise: It's those experienced innovators who have had to overcome these obstacles for years who know how to get involved and move the furniture. Find these gems – from project management, marketing, R&D, engineering, or operations – and put them on your team; they will overcome seemingly impossible barriers. Don't leave it to fresh, young "creatives" who won't know what hit them. As my dad would often say when something broke in the house, "I have two words for this situation: Hire professionals!"

With all that said, you have to know when enough is enough and a pivot isn't going to cut it.

So, when do you *stop* pivoting?

I firmly believe some of the biggest and best ideas, which usually solve category barriers, take a *long* time to solve. Those are the projects you should invest in. But you still need to deliver on the pacing of innovation for your category. So, stop pivoting on problematic small and medium innovations that are going to miss their timelines, and find a replacement project.

That could mean you delay those projects but keep working on them. Or it could mean you stop them altogether. Sometimes, these turn into zombie projects (ones that won't die!) that just aren't worth the resources required to solve their challenges. Zombie projects get delayed multiple times, never hitting their timeline. This is how organizations become known for being *slooow* and falling behind their competition. Avoid this at all costs. Keep pivoting on big bets. Have replacements in the wings for small and medium innovation, and kill the ones that start to look like zombies.

On the other end of the scale, don't get spooked by every unknown risk and try to panic pivot. If you do, you'll never get anywhere because they are limitless.

Anyone who has ever worked for me has heard me rant about unknown risks. One time, I even hung a sign on the door to my office in shouty all caps: **I DO NOT RESPOND TO UNKNOWN RISKS**. In innovation, there are *so many* things that can go wrong. But until they do, they aren't real; they are purely hypothetical problems. Technical team members – from R&D, operations/manufacturing, and engineering – are wonderful at ideating all the potential risks for a project. They are trained to think critically. That's great because it's their job to eliminate each of those risks, so the project can launch successfully. But if you are the leader of an innovation project, you have to concentrate on what *you know* and not what *you fear*. If you let these fears get in the way and spend all your time pivoting around them, you'll dismiss ideas with great potential. Negativity has a tendency to gather momentum. It's much easier to poke holes in something than to figure out how to repair it. Don't let your team fall into that trap. Do the study, the trial, the formula work, and the math ... then, if the problem is real, you can pivot.

Here's a hyperbolic example. I want to order a dress online. I think of all the unknown risks for that purchase.

- It might not fit.
- The website might be a scam.
- My credit card information might be stolen in a data breach.
- The package might get lost in the mail.
- The package could get stolen from my porch.
- The dress could arrive filled with giant ants, which then take over my neighborhood, sending children screaming in terror!

Knowing all of those risks (and I'm sure I could have thought of more), I will still order the dress. That's because the probability of any one of those things happening is low. My point is that there are risks with everything in life, but we'd never do anything new if we didn't take the leap. You have to think big and be positive – there are enough real problems to deal with without worrying about what *could* go wrong. Similarly, I never stop and pivot when I'm rearranging furniture until something is well and truly *stuck!*

But what if your company is too risk-averse to embrace this approach?

You might be willing to take that leap into the unknown, but some companies have such strict processes and such a low risk tolerance that they over-test everything before they will let it launch. When I say "test," I mean both with consumers and in manufacturing facilities. The unstated goal is to remove *all* risk before launch, whether it's a fear of unknown risks or punishing a project because it doesn't have enough scale to hit its financials immediately (even if it will in the long term if it's given the support it needs). This approach makes sense for high-risk, high-investment projects, but if it becomes a one-size-fits-all innovation process, it could cause problems. It'll force even low- and medium-risk projects to check a lot of boxes before they appear on the shelves, leading to constant delays. The reality is, this often isn't an acceptable trade-off if it creates a sluggish speed to market. The companies with the lowest risk profile move the slowest.

One solution to this is to suggest a smaller-scale launch to reduce the risk.

If you are competing in a category where you need to move quickly to keep up with the competition, this is a particularly useful strategy. For example, you could just launch in one, smaller channel or with one customer to start with. If you have the supply chain to support it, you could just launch in one region. In-market testing is so much better for reducing risk than over-testing before launch because it's not based on theoretical responses to your product. This is a last-ditch pivot to keep something on track.

But if you go down this route, I don't recommend using the standard "test market" approach (although I accept that many executives will hate this POV). This is usually when a data supplier is paid a fortune to analyze the results of launching your product in 10 stores, while comparing the results to 10 control stores that do not carry the product. So, why don't I like this?

1. **Your competition is tipped off.** The difference between the small-scale launch I suggested above and a test market is often that you aren't actually *ready* to launch. If you aren't ready to launch at scale and your idea is a big one, the competition will see your test market, copy your idea, and probably beat you to market.

2. **Test market results aren't always accurate.** You can't really advertise in the way you would nationally, so you will either A. not advertise at all, or, B. go overboard because you can afford to do that in this tiny market (I heard a story about a test market where a brand bought the billboard that was literally on top of the grocery store). In both cases, the methods will be unrealistic, undermining the results.

3. **Test markets can be *super* expensive** because you have to buy and analyze data as well as produce and distribute your product on a tiny, inefficient scale.

4. **Test markets are logistically hard to execute** (how do you get the product to just a few stores?). Solutions to this can also be expensive.

Instead, I much prefer scaling down a launch but still *launching* in the traditional sense, meaning broadly. Consider launching with just one customer but at all of their stores across the country, for example. You will learn a lot more, a lot faster, and it'll be a lot cheaper at the end of the day.

Did I lose you with all those scenarios? Here's a summary of when to pivot:

THE PIVOTING DECISION TREE

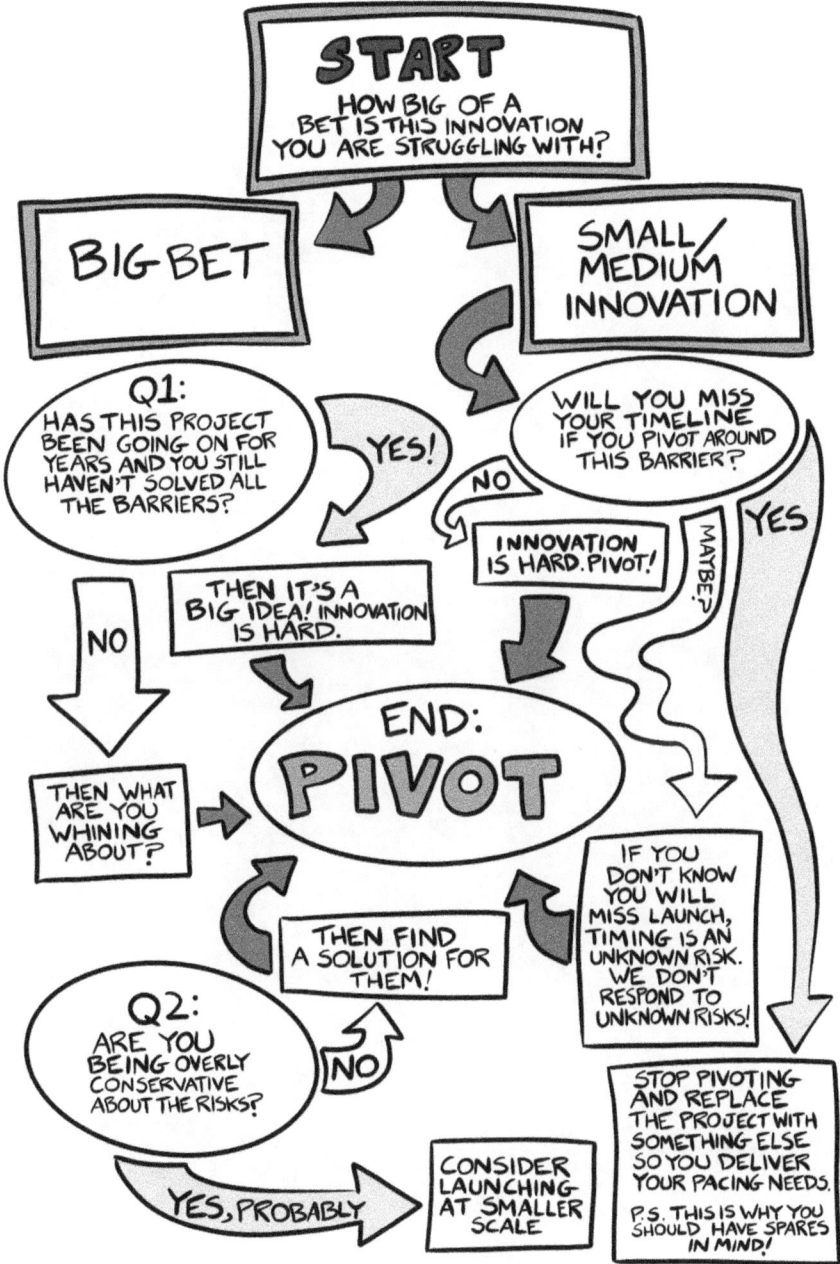

I hope that helped you think about innovation barriers differently. As I've been writing this, I've been staring at my living room and getting some ideas...

— *SNACK BREAK* —

THE SECRET INGREDIENT IN INNOVATION SUCCESS

Let's cut to the quick: A great project manager is the secret to innovation success.

They are given various names at different companies, including the project management office (PMO) or the launch program manager (LPM). If you aren't familiar with this role, they are process experts, typically trained in timeline management tools, risk identification and mitigation tactics, and cross-functional team leadership. They act as the administrative head of innovation projects. By that I mean, they effectively run the team and the project meetings, but they don't have decision rights. They are the coordinator, ensuring everyone on the project stays on track with their deliverables, so that the overall timeline is preserved.

Despite not having ownership of the idea or the product development, they are arguably the *most important member of the team*. Why? As I showed in Chapter Twelve, calendar management is critical to success. Having a full three-year calendar enables you to have flexibility to reshuffle projects when things inevitably go wrong (and they will).

A good project manager will:

- make sure new innovation projects **kick off early enough** (because, otherwise, in a world of constrained resources, teams will focus on short-term, urgent projects at the expense of long-term, harder ones).
- manage timelines tightly, **keeping projects on time**.
- **see issues or risks coming** and adjust the team's activities to address them quickly.
- know who in the organization to engage to **get decisions made or issues resolved**.

I have found that project management skills transfer across industries. I've hired PMs from automotive or IT to work in food, and they've done an excellent job. A good PM is highly disciplined and organized, collaborative, able to understand the technical project details, and at least a little bit psychic (as are all good innovators). They often have a background in engineering or operations because that skill set has a high overlap with the needs of those functions.

In short, they are worth their weight in gold.

Invest in good project managers, and your innovation program (and cost savings program!) will increase its success rate.

CHAPTER SIXTEEN

DON'T LET RENOVATION AND COST SAVINGS BRING INNOVATION DOWN

There was a period of my career where renovation – and not innovation – was the focus.

What's the difference between innovation and renovation? Innovation is about creating something new, whereas renovation is about refreshing a product that's already on the market to meet your consumers' changing expectations. It might be updating the ingredients to make it healthier or the packaging design to make it more sustainable or easier to use. (We don't usually call packaging changes designed purely to get better pricing or margin "renovation;" those are price-pack-architecture projects, or PPA.)

Anyway, in this period of my career, our key competitor invested significantly in renovation. They made product improvements designed to drive nutrition claims, which they were also shouting about in advertising and on their packaging. Management felt panicked: We were the share leader, but now we were behind the eight ball. They asked for a pipeline of product renovations consumers would want.

Our recommendation involved three major nutrition overhauls that affected a large percentage of our portfolio.

Then the rubber hit the road. Who was going to do all of this renovation work? Realistically, it would be the same people working on innovation projects. The executives looked at our well-established innovation engine – the one that had driven consistent top-line growth, the one that was certainly a big part of the reason why we had won share leadership from our key competitor – and they pillaged the calendar of innovation. A huge number of projects set to launch over the following three years were cancelled to free up resources for renovation.

The way I remember it, that decision had negative consequences on the business for the next several years. As growth slowed, stakeholders questioned what happened to all of the innovation.

Wait, you are thinking, *I thought you reinvested those resources in renovation? Didn't you drive growth that way?* Yep. We did. And, also, no. We didn't.

Because renovation doesn't drive growth, innovation does.

There. I said it. I say this all the time, and executives always argue with me. I'm sure there are some exceptions. For example, I accept there are some categories – my guesses would be automotive, paper products, and household appliances – where innovation costs billions of dollars, and therefore, truly new technologies only launch every five to 10 years. To avoid feeling stagnant, those categories need some sort of news. I can see how, in these areas, renovation might be a needed part of the mix to provide continued growth.

So, *why* doesn't renovation drive growth for the rest of us? Because it plays a different role. Renovation is *necessary* to keep up with changing consumer tastes, so it keeps you relevant to your user base, but it doesn't typically draw in *non-users*. A great example of renovation is packaging redesigns. You must do them. I mean, my goodness, think about how you feel when you see a package design that hasn't changed in 20 years. It looks so outdated. It screams to you, *I haven't kept up, I'm not what young people are looking for.* So, you have to make a change to prevent *losing* category buyers. But it won't bring new consumers to your brand on its own. It mostly keeps your current user base happy because it shows that you're still a modern brand that keeps up with trends. Everyone wants to feel that their brand is up-to-date.

For example, I don't buy crackers (except once a year when I have a holiday party). I noticed, recently, that one of the leading brands of crackers redesigned their packaging. I thought it looked really nice. But I still didn't pick it up. Because I don't buy crackers.

But this makes renovation a hard decision if you are an executive. Renovation costs money and internal resources. You want to believe it will drive growth to justify that investment. But if you lie to yourself and throw innovation out the window to make way for renovation, you will miss your top-line goals. You already know how often innovation is launching in your category if you're doing your strategy analysis. You need to keep pace with this **and** focus on renovation, so you can draw in new customers **and** keep your old customers happy.

So, my advice is to renovate as needed, but don't count on the renovation to drive growth.

I know. I'm the worst. Here, I'll throw you a lifeline.

Renovation *can* increase ad effectiveness.

Renovation makes you more modern and relevant, right? But how will people hear about this improvement? You need advertising or promotion to make the news of your renovation stand out. Otherwise, you aren't doing anything to drive growth with non-users of your product.

Where I *am* comfortable counting on growth from renovation is in your advertising effectiveness. I like this solution because it's very easy to **prove**. You should be testing your advertising messaging in some way anyway, and now you can test it with and without your renovation news and see how much more convincing it makes your ads! Then that improvement can be built into your forecast with confidence. I also recommend considering increasing the advertising spend you have in place in support of this renovation. That will drive additional growth and give you a more robust business case to justify the internal resources required to make this renovation happen. Plus, if you justify incremental resources, then you don't have to trade innovation for renovation.

What about cost savings?

You thought I'd forgotten about this part of the chapter, didn't you? Renovation, innovation, and cost savings often all use the same resources within a company. They all require product, package, or software development, financial review, and execution by manufacturing and/or sales.

For this reason, executives often want to combine cost savings and innovation. I've even seen them try to *call* cost savings "innovation," giving the word a broader meaning. That's nonsense. They drive completely different business needs! Innovation drives the top line; cost savings drive the bottom line.

Cost savings should therefore follow a *parallel but different* process to innovation within your organization.

I say parallel because cost savings follow a lot of the same processes as innovation. They need a long-term strategy with a (minimum) three-year calendar. They also need strong project management (see our last snack break!), accurate financial estimates, and clear goals.

The path may be similar, but the goals are different. Unlike innovation, which will have a goal based on your three-year innovation rate (the percentage of total revenue coming from innovation launched in the past three years – see Chapter Two for a refresher), cost savings typically aim for a total dollar savings each year or a percentage of the total cost of producing a product (often known as a COGS target = cost of goods/services sold; it just means your total cost to make something). So the goals are different. You need to hit both of those goals. Separately.

In fact, if you want to compare innovation to cost savings in order to prioritize one over the other, there's really only one effective method. That's to look at the long-term return, either through an IRR or an NPV.

IRR = internal rate of return
(The percentage you expect to earn on any company investments)

NPV = net present value
(The sum of all future cash flows less the cost of the investment)

I have worked within organizations where these metrics were used with great success to compare projects against each other. However, the challenge with using these two metrics is that the junior marketers and junior finance folks who are supporting these projects can rarely create these metrics accurately. They may not know all the discounts that go into a cash flow analysis for your company. Instead, they will likely use oversimplified assumptions that mean the metrics aren't that useful. (Also, if there is no capital or incremental marketing investment required for an innovation, an IRR is, by definition, impossible.) An automated solution in a standardized P&L template is the best solution to ensure accuracy.

Even if you *can* accurately create a list of projects ranked by NPV, it won't tell you much you don't already know. As we discussed in Chapter Three, any innovator worth their salt can rank order their project list by size, and revenue and NPV are highly correlated unless the profit on an item isn't in line with the rest of your product offerings.

So, treat your innovation and cost savings projects as separate entities. Don't try to pull resources from innovation to support cost savings. You might then hit your bottom-line goals, but you'll miss your top-line ones. And then you'll be back on the gap-closer merry-go-round.

Once you have more than you need to deliver against either your innovation or your cost savings goals, start cutting from each list appropriately. Unlike in innovation, where we kill the middle, in cost savings, you almost always just cut the tail end of the list. Those smaller projects just aren't worth the effort. If you added up the dollars you are paying to people to make the changes required to generate the savings, you will see that the tiny cost savings rarely break even.

So, what have we learned? Don't use renovation and cost savings as an excuse to kill innovation. All three have a role to play, so it's about finding a balance. You should set different goals for each, and resource each separately based on the number of projects required to hit that business need as well as their financial payback.

Innovation, cost savings, and renovation are all important. Can't we all be friends?

CHAPTER SEVENTEEN

EXECUTION MATTERS ... MOST

I want to tell you a story, but I'm going to be light on details to spare the innocent. I worked on an innovation launch that still haunts me to this day because, by all accounts, it *should* have succeeded. The idea scored better than *everything* our major research supplier had ever tested in our category before! The product was *amazing*. We spent a fortune building brand-new, shiny manufacturing lines that could run at high speeds. The financials were (or would have been) strong. We spent $50 million in advertising in year one (and this was a long time ago).

To cut a long story short, that innovation failed. Rather spectacularly, in fact. **That's the stuff of nightmares.**

The ugly truth is, an innovation can look perfect on paper. You can do everything right. But then it gets to market, and it flounders (or does an awkward and painful belly flop).

We talked about some of the modes of failure in the launch phase, *way* back in Chapter One. You might not get distribution, or you may not have enough marketing or sales support to drive trial. It might be pricing that's the problem; poor value can stop an innovation from gaining traction if consumers don't think your innovation's price is worth it compared to other offerings in your category. Your competition might launch something better at the same time. Or, even worse, they might launch something with exactly the same benefit *right before* you launch, completely wiping out your product's meaningful point of difference (which we talked about in Chapter Seven). This is part of what went wrong in my nightmare story.

But here's the interesting twist behind all this frightening risk: *The opposite is also true.* I've seen ho-hum, lackluster innovation ideas become *huge successes* in market, all because they *nailed* their execution. It's like watching someone really charismatic speak. Sometimes, they aren't even saying anything new or different, but their delivery is so powerful and emotional that it ends up being highly effective.

I'll give you a real innovation example: the launch of Velveeta Cheesy Skillets® in 2011. These were a shelf-stable boxed meal that launched into a very well-established, low-price category of boxed meals where you "just add meat." Its point of difference was that it was a liquid cheese sauce in a pouch that was ready to go instead of a powder that you had to add water or milk to.

Here's the thing. Velveeta® is an acquired taste. Some people see it as a slightly weird cheese, given it doesn't need to be refrigerated. These folks may only eat it out of politeness at their in-laws' house. But the people who buy Velveeta tend to *love* it, putting it in their dips and casseroles all the time. According to a *New York Times* article at the time of this launch, that was about 34% of Americans.[*]

So, when the innovation team tested this idea, the scores were middling at best. There was a lot of debate as to whether the innovation should

---

[*] Newman, Andrew Adam. "A Familiar Brand Promotes a New Line of Cheesy and Easy." *New York Times.* 10 Aug 2011, nytimes.com/2011/08/11/business/media/velveeta-promotes-cheesy-skillets.html.

launch. In the end, of course, it did launch. And then ... if you haven't already guessed, it performed *amazingly* in market. And it wasn't luck or a shift in the tides. It was all about the execution.

The Velveeta team did three fundamental things right:
1. They created a brilliant, breakthrough advertising campaign with strong spending behind it.
2. They won support from a top supermarket customer that drove giant displays in most of their stores.
3. They priced to appeal to economically strapped consumers who wanted cheaper at-home meal options that were higher quality.

Velveeta Cheese Skillets launched with strength. You couldn't escape this product during the launch period. The ads were everywhere. The displays were all over the stores. Go to YouTube and search "Velveeta Cheesy Skillets Liquid Gold" or "Velveeta Skillets Drive Thru" and watch the launch campaign. The blacksmith teaches Mom to "smite" her "liquid gold" dinner, holding her hands in his. It flirts with being creepy, but the actors leaned into that and made it hilarious instead. This drove a huge amount of initial trial among the Velveeta lovers. They found that third of Americans and made them sit up and listen. It was enough to make it an *enormous* success in year one.

Velveeta Skillets (rebranded) are still in the market today, 15 years later. And the brand has expanded considerably, with the addition of retort meals. It's an official success story from an innovation perspective.

Unfortunately, in my experience, Velveeta Cheesy Skillets is a bit of a unicorn. I've seen poor execution hurt innovations a lot more than I've see great execution help drive a borderline innovation to huge success.

The most common execution error that innovators make is assuming they will receive strong distribution, trade, and advertising support –

three of the key pillars of execution success – and then fail to secure what they need.

But how can you avoid this mistake? Distribution wins rely on selling your case to the gatekeepers in retail. We'll talk about these "trolls" in more detail in our next chapter. But preparation for this discussion matters. Having a strong selling story that explains why your innovation will grow the category makes all the difference to your success here.

Gaining advertising dollars or trade support for sales is about selling the story of your product internally. Too often, I see innovators assume they can get big incremental budgets. When planning time actually comes around, they get a fraction of the spending dollars that they based their forecast on. C'mon guys, let's either stop lying about our forecasts or *fight harder* to win advertising dollars from our executives. Innovation doesn't sell itself. Unless we invest to inform consumers about the unique benefits our items offer, they may never even notice that it is in market.

Small misses can add up.

So, back to the example of a failure I still think about many years later. I told you we had strong advertising spend, so that isn't where we went wrong in launch. But our point of difference was scooped by the competition, who beat us to market with a similar innovation. That made our advertising less effective; in fact, we had to scramble to create a new campaign after launch. But more importantly, we launched with one (very tiny) variety. Just one. And even though we got distribution on it, it wasn't impactful distribution. Consumers couldn't find it on the shelf. That kind of small execution miss can bring down a big idea.

Don't let off the gas at the end of the road. Push through and execute your launch with excellence.

CHAPTER EIGHTEEN

TROLLS AT THE GATE: HOW TO CONVINCE THEM TO LET YOU PASS

This is a chapter mostly about __retailers__ (although a fair bit of it could also apply to distributor partners in foodservice or other channels).

I'm going to start out by saying sorry (but not sorry) for calling retailers trolls. Sorry because I know not *all* of them are trolls. Not sorry because I feel *pretty sure* that most of them have been *trained* to be intentionally troll-like to manufacturers. I don't know whether they send all the nice, new, innocent buyers to a boot camp to toughen them up. I just know the sarcasm, impossible demands, and lectures I've experienced at the hands of retailers over the years are certainly more memorable than the pleasant, solution-oriented partnership meetings I've been part of.

I also know that, when it comes to the launch of your product innovation, retailers hold the keys to success. They control whether the launch gate opens or stays closed. That decision can make or break an innovation. Because, as you know, execution matters (most).

Your first, and most critical, need from retailers is distribution. This is getting through the gate! But that's not all. If you want a chance at success, you also need to convince them to give you strong promotional support. Ideally, this should include secondary placement outside your everyday shelf, so you can stand out and interrupt shoppers either in store or online.

So, how do you convince a troll to let you pass?

You tell an effective selling story.

We touched on this in the previous chapter, *Execution Matters …
MOST.* As an innovator, it's your responsibility to make sure the story of your innovation gets told accurately and effectively. I hate it when I

see an innovation team who – believing they've finished their part of the process – lobs the product over the wall to the sales or marketing team when it goes to market. That rarely works. *You* know the story; *you* need to tell it.

So, how do you put this together? In my experience, there are six components of an effective selling story:

1. How the innovation ties to **current market dynamics and trends** (where the growth is or where it needs to be).
2. How the innovation **targets a shopper who is attractive** to the retailer (a demographic that is growing or who spends more).
3. How the innovation will **grow the category** and not just help your brand or company (so it produces more sales for the retailer, not just for you).
4. How **consumers react to the innovation, including all the key benefits of this new offering** (this part is expected, but it may be met with skepticism, given everyone says consumers love their ideas).
5. How much **support your company is putting behind the innovation** to make sure consumers try it.
6. **BONUS:** Show how well you understand the category dynamics by **framing the entire story within a category growth framework**, explaining where growth is going to come from over the long term, not just for your brand, but for everyone. This is only a bonus step because not all companies have the sales and/or analytics resources to produce this work.

Let's look at how you might write each of these components.

1. How your innovation ties to <u>current market dynamics and trends</u>
This part can be as simple and brief as one page because the retailers are likely already aware of what's happening in the market. But it's

helpful to show that you are launching something with tailwinds and also that you understand the market dynamics. This could be about economic trends (including pricing), consumer trends, or category-specific trends. This could also be about where the category is struggling or behind, as a lead-in to how this innovation will help.

2. The shopper you are targeting

This section needs to be *customized* for each retailer. Are they trying to bring younger shoppers in? Or more affluent shoppers? Explain how your innovation will help them achieve this and how your goals are aligned with theirs. Don't use your own internal, gimmicky marketing terms around your target consumers. You need to read the documents they share about their own growth strategy and then translate your target consumer into their language, so it resonates. And remember that relatable stories matter. Don't just name the target shopper; *describe them* and their needs. Help the buyer picture their own family, friends, and neighbors.

3. How it will grow the category

This is a test of how much you've considered the channel strategy throughout your innovation project. Hopefully, you aren't launching "me too" innovation that just closes a gap for *your brand* by launching something that already exists in the market. Ideally, you've thought about solving consumers' unmet needs. If you have, *explain that!* What does this innovation do for the retailer's shoppers?

In this section, you need to explain *why* you created this innovation. And support that with any data you have about how incremental you expect it to be.

4. How consumers react to it

Now the big reveal. You've set the stage with the trends you are targeting, the people you are targeting, and the problem to be solved.

At this point, you can share how excited consumers are about your offering and what *exactly* it is.

What are all the benefits? How is it packaged? How is it priced? And what did consumers say about all of those details?

Here's the thing. Trolls – sorry, retailers – hearing about the great scores an innovation receives, will often say, "Yeah, everyone tells me their ideas are good," or, "You always say this." But I still think it's important to share your data, especially to overcome any personal opinions they may have about your idea (or worse, their families: "My son doesn't like these"). If you can show that a huge percentage of people surveyed loved it, you should.

5. The <u>support</u> your company will put behind it

Showing your company is betting big on an innovation is a great selling point. If something will be heavily advertised, no retailer will want to pass on it because they know consumers will be looking for it in stores or on their website. A statistic I love to use in a selling story is the percentage of target shoppers who you expect to see your advertising (it is often high!).

Also, show them a draft of the trade plan behind the idea ... this makes it clear how much you are investing to promote the item and drive trial.

The media landscape is changing fast, but at the time of publication, retail media (search, aka sponsored placements or ads bought at fill-in-your-retailer.com) is an important driver of sales and very motivating to buyers. Right now, I would say that is the first dollar you should consider spending (if you can get to scale). And use this as a negotiation tactic to get what you want from retailers, i.e., "We will spend X if you give us Y."

6. BONUS: Frame your story within a <u>category growth framework</u>

If your company has a strong selling organization, you may already have a category-specific story for retailers that focuses on the key drivers of growth. If this hasn't been created for the company as a whole, your field sales teams for bigger retailers may have one they've developed.

If one exists, *leverage it*. Frame your innovation within it. It's a great chance to reinforce the fact that you are a manufacturer who understands the market dynamics you compete in. And it shows the retailer you are trying to help them grow their business as well as your own.

If one doesn't exist, and this is a really big bet innovation, consider pulling together a team within marketing, sales, and analytics to create one. A good growth-drivers story will really improve your credibility with a troll, and it might make them less gruff.

Okay, so now you've got a strong selling story. What now? Don't just throw that over the wall to sales. Offer to show up!

I think innovators should personally sell their innovations to the top five retailers in their business category, at a minimum. If you can book an in-person or virtual meeting with a retail buyer dedicated to a new item discussion, that is ideal. So, prepare for some travel! You know the innovation better than anyone, and your passion for it will bring energy to the discussions. Give those trolls in retail so many reasons to say yes that you overcome that boot camp training they (allegedly) got about being big meanies to manufacturers.

Execution matters (most), so put as much energy into winning the distribution of your product as you did into the rest of the development process.

— *SNACK BREAK* —

FAIL <u>FASTER</u> AND INTERVENE

We all have that uncle who's really bad at telling jokes. The kind of person who starts to tell a joke then can't remember exactly how it goes and tries to paraphrase or explain the punchline, diverting off on tangents to tell you little, unimportant details. The joke itself might be fantastic, but the delivery is terrible.

Sigh The worst part is this uncle usually laughs the whole time they are rambling on because they know what happens in the joke. In contrast, you are just sitting there, staring into space, with a polite half smile on your face, thinking, *What. On. Earth. Are we talking about right now?*

The simple fact is, at this point, there's no recovering.

Jokes are all about timed delivery. No second chances.

Product innovation is the same.

If your innovation is failing, you need to react *fast* because there are no second chances. Your window of opportunity is small. Consumers, retailers, and your own executives will not patiently wait for your innovation to deliver the way you wait for your uncle to get to the punchline.

I've found that if a product flounders, you have about nine to 18 months to get it back on track, or it's over. Maybe not over *forever* – really good ideas that solve actual consumer problems tend to come back – but usually not for another five to 10 years. Which, funnily enough, is roughly the memory span of your executives and retailers – and they likely won't bet on a loser twice. So, if your innovation is going off track, and you don't want to wait five to 10 years to relaunch it, you need to fail faster, one way or another.

Here's how the <u>fail slow</u> trap plays out:
- Innovators set unrealistic forecasts (e.g., they lie to get something launched);
- The innovation comes out of the gate much weaker than those expectations;
- Marketing and sales try to pass off these misses as "too early to read";
- By the time it's clear the project is way off track, you are too late to fix it before the nine- to 18-month timer is up and your innovation is toast.

But what does failing faster mean? You must have realistic and well-communicated (internal) expectations for how distribution, trial, and repeat will grow over your first and second year in market. These phased targets should be based on recent innovation in your category that is similarly sized. Then you need to religiously track against those metrics … starting no later than week three.

Failing faster essentially has two steps: 1. Intervene instantly, and 2. know when to fold.

1. Intervene instantly

If you have accurate and realistic forecasts for distribution and trial, it is *never* "too early" to intervene. You should have been tracking retailer/distributor acceptances by point of distribution, and if you aren't getting them, sales should be making phone calls, asking for meetings, and pitching your amazing sell story. If you have a broker, they can even try to sell at store level in some cases.

If this is a big bet, *never be afraid to ask for more investment early on*. Ask for sales spending to drive deeper discounts and displays. Ask for marketing spending to invest in trial-driving tactics with high, fast returns. This isn't throwing good money after bad ... the investment made to date on a big bet will have been years of people time, in addition to the capital and marketing spend already committed. Can you imagine buying a new home and then refusing to fix a water leak? Do your best to make your innovation work. If you can't understand what is going wrong, I recommend doing a fast, cheap consumer survey among triers to understand how they feel about your product.

2. Know when to fold

If you find you've made a fundamental mistake on an innovation and that is why it's off to a slow start – the product isn't well-received, the value is way off vs. the market, the placement of your item isn't right, your benefit isn't meaningful, or some other major miss – it is sometimes better to know when to fold and take it off the shelves. Yes, it's heartbreaking. But a lot of innovation fails. You need a strong stomach to be an innovator, both personally and as a company.

You will get credit, both internally with leadership and externally with your customers, for openly admitting the mistakes an innovation has made and how your team is learning from them. Retailers will certainly be frustrated with the wasted effort on their part (cutting new items onto shelf and into warehouses comes with expense), but I find transparency about your learning goes over better than forcing them to be the troll who tells you your new item sucks.

Finally, knowing the *why* is crucial for both of these steps

The earlier you know why your innovation is failing, the better chance you have of intervening, and the more likely you are to improve your innovation success going forward.

Knock, knock.

Who's there?

Not your uncle, hopefully.

CHAPTER NINETEEN

THE BORING BUSINESS CHAPTER: THE FUNDAMENTALS OF INNOVATION SUCCESS

Ahh, the boring business chapter. This chapter is for people who *like* business books. Thanks for getting this far ... and sorry for the cussing earlier.

This book was written for innovators. I mean for it to be a guide to how to overcome some of the most common obstacles in innovation. But **this chapter is for business leaders.** If you are trying to start an innovation program, or fix a broken one, here is what you need to think about: the fundamentals of innovation success. But what are they?

1. Strategy
2. People
3. Process
4. Financials
5. Execution

These are the foundation of an innovation program. If you are missing one of them, you will probably fail. If you are failing, you are probably missing one of them.

1. STRATEGY

In Chapter Thirteen, I talked about how to write an innovation strategy. That's key, but it's not everything. I want you to answer these questions honestly. They will help you to understand what you need to build a strong strategy that supports innovation.

- Do you have a **clear innovation consumer or customer target?**
- Do you understand their needs? Is the innovation pipeline being **built against target insights?**
- Do you have **clear objectives** for innovation? (We'll talk about financials later in this chapter; here, I mean what is the innovation going to do for your business more broadly?)
- Does the innovation strategy clearly **tie back to the overall business strategy?** What about the total company strategy?
- Are you **innovating against areas of strength** for you, or are you trying to use innovation to shore up areas of weakness? (See Chapter Two, *What Innovation Success Really Looks Like,* and the snack break right before it, *Innovation Won't Fix Your Broken Business,* if so.)

I keep saying "clear," and that's essential. Clear means not only easy for everyone to understand but also understood by *everyone.* Meaning it's something you talk about with the broader team. Innovation is a team sport, and you need to have each other's backs when the going gets tough. If only a few leaders understand what the role of innovation is in the broader growth agenda, your program will probably fail. That's because different functions will have different goals in their own minds. You need one, unifying strategic understanding to keep everyone rowing in the same direction.

2. PEOPLE

In order to generate a healthy mix of big bet, medium, and small product innovation, you'll need dedicated people. By dedicated, I mean they should be completely ring-fenced for innovation, so they don't end up focusing on other, shorter-term priorities. From experience, if you want a well-rounded and complete innovation program, **you'll need dedicated roles in R&D, project management, consumer insights/research, marketing, and finance**. Ideally, you would also throw in a dedicated engineering role or two, especially if you want to do bigger innovation involving capital or changes to your manufacturing processes.

You might be thinking: *Isn't this the innovation island you warned us against in Chapter Nine?* That's absolutely not what I mean by "dedicated." These people should still report into each of their respective functional business teams, so they maintain strong communications and links to the business strategy. It's about creating the *focus* that innovation needs.

Dedicating people to the innovation team is a first big step, but sometimes, a harder shift is **ensuring your new team has the right cultural environment to be successful**. Company culture can be deeply engrained and difficult to change.

Ask yourself the following:
- Do you have a culture that embraces acceptable levels of risk and the potential for failure?
- Do you have a culture patient enough to focus on long-term goals, which is essential for big-ticket innovation?
- Are mid-level leaders in key innovation functions like marketing and R&D empowered to take risks and make decisions?
- Is the senior leadership team and board supportive? Are they aligned with the innovation strategy? Do they approve of

investment in innovation, and do they encourage risk taking for future growth?

- Are innovation roles respected? Is there a career path to them and beyond them? (I've worked in places where innovation was perceived as for the head-in-the-clouds "creative people," or worse, was downgraded as the role for those looking for easy or part-time work, often seen as "for moms" … *don't* get me started on that.)

Culture is key. If innovators have to swim against the tide of how your company thinks and/or acts, you will only succeed with a full team of very bold, brave people. That's hard to find. If these questions give you pause, consider engaging HR or change management experts to help coach your innovation team, or more broadly, to start changing your total company culture.

3. PROCESS

When people think about innovation processes, they go right to the stage-gate system. And they aren't wrong. I haven't seen a better process for managing innovation. It provides a clear set of gates at the end of each stage, where innovation teams must stop and get leadership alignment and approval to keep going. That ensures projects have the support they need and don't get off track.

So, if you don't have a gate process, get on that; every innovation process should begin with this foundation. But innovation process goes much further than this.

Here are some other process levers to consider:
- Do you have a **prioritization process**? How do you decide where to put innovation resources? How much is too much? (See Chapter Three for my thoughts on prioritization of innovation.)
- Do you have a **way to engage sales in innovation**? Is that process

clear and consistent? Is it happening early and often enough?

- Are there **clear KPIs (key performance indicators) for innovation,** both before and after launch? Are those KPIs automated and tracked? Knowing the three to five key numbers we need innovation to hit is critical to making the gates *actual* gates (and not those fancy fake gates people who live on major roads put up but never close). This might be things like revenue minimums, margin targets, or launch timing.

- Do you have a **process for creating, approving, and reviewing a three-year innovation calendar?** A built-out long-term pipeline is a key component of innovation success. I find it helpful to have an annual planning process that mirrors the strategic planning process for the whole business (the results of which are often called annual operating plans or AOPs) but is dedicated to the innovation process. This gives the innovation team clear timelines for when they are expected to bring next year's ideas forward for alignment with the executive team.

- Is there a **clear path to market for innovation,** without surprises? How do projects transfer from innovation to the people who run the business every day? How do they transfer to sales? Operations? No one should be surprised as your innovation moves from being a project to being a product because lots of collaboration should have happened from the very beginning.

As you evaluate your innovation processes, also **evaluate your speed to market.** Are you keeping up with competition? Do you need to review (or maybe create) standard timelines for innovation to see where your team is getting bogged down? Finding the pinch points will tell you where you might need additional resources and/or leadership intervention to keep things going.

In product innovation, the most common pinch points are in idea alignment with marketing, (over) testing, product development (especially when understaffed), legal/regulatory approval, and engineering. You'll want to find the right balance between the rigor appropriate for your risk tolerance and the speed you need to succeed. You can usually go a lot faster if leadership is willing to trust the experience of the team and lean in on some risk.

4. FINANCIALS

When I say "financials," you may think I am just talking about P&Ls. I'm not.

A successful innovation program requires the following financial tools, funding, and support:
- Standardized P&L tools
- Clear margin goals (see Chapter Four)
- Forecasting tools (see Chapter Five)
- Insights funding
- Brainstorm funding
- R&D research funding
- Allocated capital spending (or development of a strong contract manufacturing network)
- Advertising and trade support in market

To save you time, I'm not going to repeat the ones I've already explained at length in other chapters. But I'll do a quick dive into the other financial considerations.

Let's start with **standardized P&Ls**. I can't tell you how many times I have started working on a new business only to discover P&Ls for innovation were being created ad hoc, in blank Excel files, with no consistent format. This is a recipe for disaster. Your company should have a standard format that all innovators use to lay out the financials for their innovation. It should start with the expected revenue and then list expected trade rates, product costs, and resulting margins. It should calculate the impact of cannibalization, so the incrementality of the innovation is considered. Ideally it should also list expenses like capital depreciation and advertising and include an NPV and/or IRR calculation of that investment. Consistency in these calculations is imperative to enable accurate comparison and prioritization across innovation projects. If you don't have a standardized innovation P&L, get a small group of finance experts together and create one.

If you've read the previous chapters, **insights funding** should be a no-brainer. Keeping the consumer at the center of your innovation process is key to identifying big, incremental ideas that will drive true growth. Relying on our own opinions and experiences, or those of our family and friends, is a *bad idea*. Why? Because most corporate employees working on innovation projects are privileged in multiple ways. For instance, they're probably in the top 5% of income brackets in their area. They are also much more educated (less than half of adults in the U.S. have a college degree, according to the U.S. Census Bureau[**]), and they likely have much more exposure to the rest of the world than the average citizen. Your innovators (and their friends and families) simply don't represent the average consumer. So. You need to spend money on consumer research, or you'll probably miss the mark. What leaders sometimes don't think about is the cost of that essential work.

Brainstorming funding needs to be part of the innovation budget. Having the option to rent a creative space, engage a moderator, and invite (and pay) non-employee experts will all lead to more disruptive ideas. You may also need external help, meaning fees to bring in innovation consultants or agencies with Agile experience that think completely differently and can provide you with new ideas and brainstorm approaches.

[**] U.S. Census Bureau, American Community Survey, 2023. data.census.gov/table?q=DP02R

Funding the 'R' part of R&D is also key to a successful innovation program. You hired scientists and engineers with expertise in your product category for a reason; you don't just want "developers." Make sure you have dedicated people set aside to do **true research**. If you are small, this may just be one person working on technologies that are still three or more years out from feasibility. If you are big, you probably want a whole team. They should have a clear, aligned road map of technologies they are pursuing. And they should work with universities and suppliers on advancing those technologies. Importantly, they should check in with leadership once a quarter on their progress. This will ensure your researchers are staying tight to that road map ... and that they feel some time pressure to make progress. (Without all of this, your research team may drift off to become the innovation island I described in Chapter Nine.)

Capital is another tricky investment area for innovation. It's tricky because it involves something CFOs don't always like to hear – that you should dedicate a portion of your annual capital budget to innovation. And I don't mean find out what is needed and roll that into the capital plan. I mean *earmark* money for projects that may or may not yet be identified. Why? It sends a message. When there is money *held* for innovation, it tells the entire team that 1. you *expect* innovation to cost money, and 2. it's a key part of your corporate strategy. Otherwise, I find project teams will often compromise or kill good ideas because they *assume* there's no room in the budget for capital spending. They are afraid to ask for an amount they perceive to be a *lot* of money. But, the truth is, what a junior innovator sees as a *lot* of money is not often a lot of money to a company, especially if it has a good return and drives incremental growth (which big capital innovations usually do!). Earmarking money removes that barrier, making innovators more likely to think big.

If you can't commit capital, then you need to develop a strong contract manufacturing network. These co-manufacturers need to have more flexibility for innovation than your existing production facilities. Or they need to be willing to invest the capital in innovation themselves and charge it back to you in your cost of goods.

Finally, advertising and trade support are not optional "nice to haves." They are essential to your success. Why invest all that time and money in dedicated innovation teams, brainstorming, insights, and testing and then *tell no one* about your new product?

Trade will help to drive new product trial through displays, promotions, and price incentives, and advertising will drive high levels of awareness and trial behind your innovation as well. It's important to know the purchase cycles for your category and advertise across more than just one cycle. A purchase cycle is the number of days, weeks, months, or years that pass between purchases for your consumer. If you are talking about cars, it's probably *years*. You'll need to advertise a new car model across that period. If you are talking about fast food items, it could be weeks. If you only advertise your new item for one or two purchase cycles, you may not drive enough trial. So, make sure you invest sufficiently.

5. EXECUTION

The final piece of the innovation fundamentals puzzle is execution. As I said in Chapter Seventeen, execution is often *more* important than the idea itself in predicting innovation success. That's why advertising matters so much.

If you are a senior leader setting up an innovation program, you should ponder the following:

- How are your handoffs to sales working? Do you have **strong selling stories** being jointly created across marketing and sales to communicate the consumer story in a way your customers will understand and buy into (if not, go back and review Chapter Eighteen, which details how to create one)?

- Is there a process **to closely track in-market acceptance** among retailers or distributors before launch?
- Is there a process to **closely track in-market performance** after launch? Does it catch weak launches quickly enough so you can pivot and try to fix them?
- Is there a consistent **pattern to how your innovations fail?** Are you sharing learning from failures to make sure they're not repeated?
- How effective are your **manufacturing startups** for product innovations? Are you doing enough trials in advance to ensure a smooth startup?
- How is your **product quality** at startup?
- How **effective is your supply chain** at startup? Are you shipping to customers on time?

Don't just grab your keys and trip out the door with your innovations. Make sure they have the very best chance to succeed.

Optimize those five pillars – strategy, people, process, financials, and execution – and you'll give your innovation team a path toward beating the odds. Miss a key component of even one, and you'll almost guarantee their failure.

CHAPTER TWENTY

A GRACEFUL EXIT

Somehow, we made it to the end of the book. This is the last chapter. We're finally leaving the haunted-house horror show that is innovation. And we didn't even have to run out of the emergency exit (I hope). You've pivoted around barriers, left and right, and escaped the winds of innovation change.

But before I wrap this up, I want to talk about something very important: **what do when innovation fails**. Because, if you are an innovator, you *will* work on something that fails. It's part of the gig.

You may not want to think about the prospect of your project going up in flames. Talking about innovation projects, people always compare them to "babies," saying, "Oh, that's *her* baby," or, "Don't call his baby ugly!"

But innovations aren't babies that need to be coddled. They are soldiers that must fight for their lives. Innovation is like warfare. You have to keep sending troops into battle with your competition, and you have to accept that they might not all make it. That's the ugly truth.

I've had that feeling of dread so many times. You start seeing the numbers come in on a launch, and they aren't where they should be.

Slowly, you begin to realize this one isn't going to make it. You get asked to explain. After nurturing your innovation for so long, it's so easy to let the emotions take over and become defensive ... because failure is scary. Even in a culture that accepts the risk of innovations failing, it's not what anyone wants.

Here's my advice to you on how to behave with both intelligence and grace if your innovation is failing:

1. **Accept failure as a team, and learn from it**
   - It doesn't matter whose fault it is. *Never* play the blame game.
   - But it is important to understand all the whys. Keep a team mindset as you search for those answers and support each other.
   - We must learn from our mistakes as a company to keep from repeating them.

2. **Share your learning broadly**
   - Don't let others tell your story. If you led an innovation, take ownership of and accountability for the failure, and explain the whys.
   - Don't just share within the tight innovation team, either; make sure the whole business team knows what you've learned.
   - It's especially important to share learning with sales and give them a summary they can share with their customers. Sales teams often feel *they* are blamed when innovation fails. That's because they own a lot of the final execution elements of the launch, including distribution, pricing, and promotion. They are also typically asked to "sign up" for the volume in your new item forecast, so initially, when the project is missing target, they will feel the heat from executives to explain the miss by customer. If there are modes of failure impacting the

project that were outside of sales' control, it's important to acknowledge this and share it with them.

• You may feel like being honest with your customers and distributors about why something didn't work will make you vulnerable. In reality, they will become more trusting and confident in your ability to deliver future innovation if you show you are able to reflect and iterate to improve your approach. Accountability builds trust.

3. **Don't let one failure ruin the whole plan or process**

• Sometimes, organizations get spooked by a failure and start questioning the whole innovation strategy or process. Or worse, the innovation team. Strategy *could* be the problem … but remember all the modes of innovation failure from Chapter One? There are so many different causes other than strategy, so don't jump to conclusions.

• If you feel confident that the overall plan and process are robust, make any changes that are necessary based on your analysis of the failure, and stick to your guns on everything else. Remember that starting over will cause a gap in innovation the length of your development time (often years). Try to reassure your leadership that you have learned and adjusted and there is no reason to pendulum swing away from your innovation engine.

• Most importantly, don't fall prey to panic. Stay optimistic. You have to believe to succeed in innovation.

In case you've forgotten, innovation is ugly.

It takes a certain amount of tenacity to be an innovator and ride the rollercoaster. We don't stop often enough to recognize that in ourselves. We are brave!

Some people will give up on hard things. Because they are afraid to fail and be punished, because they don't have support, or because they don't feel ownership of their work, which eats into their motivation. Or maybe just because they aren't having fun anymore.

I hope this book has helped you feel more confident to navigate the challenges innovation throws our way – to feel less afraid and to take control of and drive support for your projects. I hope that it has empowered you to take the lead in this dynamic and exciting (and challenging and infuriating) area and have fun while you are doing it. Most of all, I hope reading this book has helped you feel less alone. I hope you have felt seen and supported. Innovation is hard, and often innovators don't have leaders with the experience to coach them through tough times.

I certainly had fun writing this, and I hope it didn't feel like your average – boring – business book. If you have any feedback or want to talk about innovation, I'd love to hear from you at:

Innovationisugly@gmail.com

THANK-YOUS

I hate the paragraph thank-yous that usually appear in books. Don't people just want a list they can skip through to see if they know anyone … or made the cut themselves?! I like bullet points.

My endless gratitude to:

- **Kaitlin,** my only and quite perfect daughter. Without her support and encouragement, I never would have finished (or even started) this book. She knew I could do it, and she's always right. Kaitlin, you are the funniest and most fun part of my life, always. Here's to many more hilarious stories I will twist.

- **Sarah Busby,** my editor, who gave me SO MUCH confidence in my ability to make this book happen, and who erased MOST of the shouty all caps in my original draft. :) This book is so much stronger and clearer thanks to Sarah's guidance; she even researched baseball to make sure I wasn't screwing up those (angry) analogies.

- My graphic illustrator, **Dave Fakes,** who made this manuscript look really *ducking* unique. I didn't want traditional, straight-lined tables and charts, and his talent with characters also inspired me to add lots of them. I hope my readers love them as much as I do.

- My cover illustrator and interior designer **Victoria Heath Silk,** who was willing to go on a journey to create a "scary" business book with me. Thanks for bringing your innovative thinking to the process. I'm so happy with where we landed!

- **My six brothers and sisters, Cathy, Mary, Judy, Sadie, Matt, and Pat, and my sister-in-law, Timberly,** for helping me become the bossy and accomplished bitch I am today, whether they intended to or not. I'm so proud of what *you* have accomplished in your lives. Thanks for being the seven best friends anyone could ever hope for; I know we always have each other's backs through good times … and slightly-more-dramatic times.

- **My mom and dad,** who have kept our big, crazy family united as *one team*. Mom taught me to push hard for what I need and to love harder. Dad taught me to balance serious leadership and decision-making with complete, genuine silliness. And my stepmom Marie values family as much as we do, and we are all grateful to her for that.

- **Risa Duesing,** my best friend in insights, who keeps me from getting a big head by constantly reminding me that most of the things that go wrong in my life are my fault. Her antics makes me laugh so hard, but she is also always there when I'm struggling.

- **Kim Harvey, Angela Gusse, Shirley Chambliss, Elizabeth Obbard, Roxanne Bernstein, and my departed but not forgotten friend Beth Healy,** who have been my cheerleaders in life and the people I can always lean on in tough times. I don't deserve them, but I am so grateful to have found them. Their strength continues to inspire my own.

- My cousin **Andy Balas,** who left this world too early, but not before teaching me so many lessons about love, laughter and butt wipes, specifically. (IYKYK)

- **Jen Bentz and Andy Callahan,** who both took chances on me and stretched me to be bigger and better. I owe much of my career success to the two of you.

- **Eric Pfieffer, Liz Gillis (rest in peace), Hana Kim, Heather Boggs, Russell Thomas, Tam Grall, Darryl Riley, and Cherie Floyd, among others,** who taught me the value of the Venn diagram, by being both my polar opposites and my dear friends in innovation. I would never have survived without all the laughs we had together.

- **To my early readers, Julie Ketay, Elizabeth Obbard, and Nicole Sorensen.** Thanks most of all for your encouragement! It meant so much to me you took the time to read this and send suggestions.

- **All the women, minorities, LGBTQ+ community members, disabled persons, and other outsiders** struggling to break the many glass ceilings of corporate America. Never give up on who you are or who you want to be. Find people who believe in you and cling to their encouragement. And know that while *not fitting in* is painful, if we want anything to change, it's also *the point.* Take up space.

Finally, to all innovators who keep on keeping on, even when it's the bottom of the 9th with two outs and you hate baseball analogies. Pivot, baby, pivot. It's all worth it when the growth stacks up. And try to have some freakin' fun.

ABOUT THE AUTHOR

Tina Lambert has spent over 25 years as a marketer and innovator across both Fortune 500 and smaller, high-growth companies. In that time, she's tried her level best to drive growth, pivot around barriers, and build innovation teams that love their jobs.

Tina lives in Chicago, Illinois, near her two best friends in insights, one of her (awesome) six siblings, and with a couple of high-maintenance dogs that *hate* how little attention they get when she's writing.

She has still not been back in a haunted house.

www.ingramcontent.com/pod-product-compliance
Lightning Source LLC
Chambersburg PA
CBHW021921190326
41519CB00009B/870